The Truth and Love Journey

Experience the Secrets of Life-Giving Relationships

VINCENT NELSON & BETHANY WILLIAMS

Carpenter's Son Publishing

Published by Carpenter's Son Publishing, Franklin, Tennessee

Published in association with Larry Carpenter of Christian Book Services, LLC
www.christianbookservices.com

Interior and Cover Design by Suzanne Lawing

Edited by OnFire Books

Copy Edit by Lee Titus Elliott

Printed in the United States of America

978-1-949572-97-1

CONTENTS

DEDICATION

We're Christ's representatives. God uses us to persuade men and women to drop their differences and enter into God's work of making things right between them. We're speaking for Christ himself now: Become friends with God; he's already a friend with you."
2 CORINTHIANS 5:20 (MSG)

This book you have in your hands today is our passion. This is our purpose. May the pages of this book transform your relationships, erase loneliness, and eliminate despair. May your journey through life, as you learn how to receive, live in truth, and love with your Creator, yourself and others, empower you to experience the deepest peace, the warmest embrace, and set you off on the path to living your purpose with others.

To our children Nick, Simon, Heather, Brandon, and Caleb and their spouses and significant others Brian, Bailey, and Shelbey and the legacy we leave with you.

May the wisdom we've learned through the darkest moments of our lives become light for your own journey. The greatest gift we could ever give you, even in the midst of our greatest failures as human beings and parents, is that you learn freedom is found in receiving, not striving. Learning to be vulnerable and truthful with yourselves and others gives you the greatest opportunity to discover true intimacy and real life...being fully known, knowing the other in your life fully, and being deeply embraced. We wish for you the most amazing relationships you could ever experience. We hope the pages of this book become a road map for you on your own truth and love journey.

FOREWORD
Tammy Kling

How healthy are your relationships? This might seem like a challenging question, but since you picked up this book, it's a relevant one. True wealth can be measured by the depth, trust, and openness of the relationships you have with others.

I've worked with a lot of world changers in my life, including the CEOs of some of the world's greatest companies, entrepreneurs you see on television, athletes, and celebrities. I've put these amazing humans on our TEDx stage and interviewed hundreds of humanitarians and leaders for their books. But I can honestly say that the authors of this book that you hold in your hands are two of the most authentic humans I've ever met.

When you meet them you know that there's nothing contrived or false about their message. They deliver truth and bare their souls here on these pages, even when it makes them uncomfortable.

After years of working with amazing authors to bring their message and books to the world, I can tell you that the journey itself to even tell their story requires a lot of courage. And this is what I want to leave behind with you today. No matter what it is you're facing, please believe that you can face it and you will. You don't have to face anything joyfully, you don't have to put on a mask or a smile, all you have to do is reach deep inside to find the courage within you.

Be strong and courageous.

Whatever you're facing in life and business will eventually require courage.

Chi Chi Rodriguez, a legendary professional golfer who donated much of his winnings to orphans, told me that you cannot be courageous without adversity. He sat in my living room one day and shared the stories of his life, from the moment he was a child without shoes, who first stepped onto a golf course in Puerto Rico. Chi Chi had no shoes until the age of twelve or so. Imagine the courage it took to step into a rich man's game, on a wealthy golf course, and compete.

You cannot have courage without some sort of challenge or adversity.

I thought about that statement for months after he left my house, and it's true. Courage is like a weapon. It's a tool to step forward and fight whatever we are facing with valor, even if we feel fear.

Extreme challenge in life or relationships requires courage.

Intimacy, and a close, honest, and open relationship with another human, requires courage. For some of us it's easier to tackle massive problems, build companies, and handle a crisis than it is to look someone in the eye, sit still, and talk about things of the heart. I suspect it's not just the high achievers who can be intimacy avoiders, but those who have been hurt or betrayed or made fun of, too.

This reminds me of a girl I once knew who threw away long-term relationships the moment her partner criticized her or called her out on something. Relationships are give-and-take, blunt truth, and conversations rooted in love. But when she sensed that her mate was angry or disappointed, she just left rather then dealing with it.

Dealing with conflict requires courage. Conflict resolution is for big boys and girls and not for the weak of heart.

Vince and Bethany remind each one of us that moments of discomfort are merely the building blocks of a substantial character.

Discomfort requires you to listen.

Discomfort requires you to apologize.

Discomfort requires you to be vulnerable and share your fears, your pet peeves, and your temptations and struggles. They use the word intimacy, but I'll add another critical element of business and love relationships here—transparency.

The ability to be transparent and uncomfortable is the mark of strong character and maturity.

Give me a friend who is truthful any day over one who is passive aggressive and doesn't state their needs. When a friend or mate says one thing and they really mean another, are they telling you the truth?

Transparency is a sign of respect. The ones you love deserve your honesty.

I have a strange track record for match making, by hearing God speak, that's resulted in several marriages including this one. Nick Vujicic, and his wife met in my home and so did Vince and Bethany and several others. It's a gift of connectivity, really, but it works only because I'm bold enough to be honest and share what I hear. Had I not shared with Vince when I heard the name "Bethany," I never would've put them together as a couple because I barely knew her and Vince was a total stranger at the time who had called me and signed up for coaching.

No matter who you are or where you are in your life, you will benefit from their story. Reading this book will give you insight into your own relationships and encourage you that the best may be yet to come. There are second and third chances! Today is the day to step out on faith. Let's do this together and commit to a more transparent, honest, and loving year. Let's commit to communicating our love or gratitude every day by telling someone we love exactly what it is we love about them. Let's make a pact to create intentionality about deeper relationships.

Be strong and courageous.
JOSHUA 1:9 (NIV)

PROLOGUE

The Journey's Beginning

In the pages of this book you'll find one of the greatest treasures this world has to offer, which is the gift of true and lasting intimacy. Intimacy with others is fuel for humanity.

Like water and food are essential for us to exist, intimate human relationships are energy for the soul, birthing some of the greatest songs, paintings, and poems the world has ever known. By deep family relationships, great leaders have been able to stand strong against opposition and be true to their purpose. Deep friendships have helped many overcome difficult times. The fundamental need of the human soul is to be loved, understood, accepted, and to reach out to do the same.

We want to invite you to experience that for your own life. The only way we know how to do that is by doing the very thing that creates intimacy in the first place, being deeply vulnerable. We might have changed some names to protect the families associated with those names, but everything else shared in these pages that are filled with brutal truth. You will read stories of failure, shame, loss, deep brokenness, and surrendered hearts.

Have you ever been hurt or betrayed by someone you love? Chances are the answer is yes. Humans are human.

We're inviting you on our very transparent journey because we want you to know that no matter how badly you've been hurt and have retreated from authentic relationships, or no matter the destruction you've caused yourself or others in life, there is still hope for you. No matter what you've done or haven't done, no matter how badly you've messed up, you can experience deep lifelong intimacy.

Where do we start?

The first thing to know is that the journey towards intimacy is messy, very hard, and downright painful at times. As a matter of fact, it's often extremely ugly because it's a journey that starts with your own inward soul. It requires no longer running away and burying your past shame, pain, and failures in the busyness of life. It requires great courage for it's a journey that requires reflection on your past, healing from sometimes life long wounds and courage to step out knowing you are lovable and worth it.

If you cringe just reading those words, its a sign you need this journey.

Once you've gotten to the place where you understand that YOU really have amazing value and a unique purpose, it's then you can begin the journey of experiencing intimacy with another person. If you've not dealt with past relational wounds, and loss, then we invite you to start with Vince's book *Child of the King*. As you journey through the pages of his book, you'll find the courage to face your past, find healing, and discover the magnificent value your Creator has already given you. As you begin to walk in that newfound sense of worth and start to live your unique purpose, you'll find you're ready to experience deep relationships with others.

If you're just ready to dive in, let's go. We are with you on this journey.

How do you sum up thirty-six years of failures in brevity? In parts of this book you may hear pieces of the past that had imprisoned both of us. In revealing those failures, we realize many will try to put us in prisons of judgement and condemnation. We can accept what others may think now that we've received God's love and forgiveness and our own forgiveness for all our failures and for the pain we've caused others.

While this book is written for the purpose of experiencing intimacy with your dating partner leading to lifelong marriage and to enhance your marital relationship, it's something that can apply to all relationships. Whether you've never been married or you're a second-chance single (we love second-chance singles because you have a unique opportunity for discovering and living your purpose with a like-minded person), you'll find there's incredible hope ahead. It simply starts with having the courage to make the journey.

Think of it like climbing a mountain where a beautiful summit awaits you. To get there, you'll have to make some difficult steps to traverse cliffs, climb over boulders, and hike for miles when you are dog tired. Don't give up, your reward is ahead—the incredible summit of lasting intimacy with another. It begins with the journey of the inward soul that ultimately will lead to the journey of outward healthy relationships. Join us in the pages of this book on the journey of discovering the kind of intimacy where it's safe to be you. It's a place of deep vulnerability where you are fully known and know the other person fully and find you are completely loved and embraced. We believe in you and know you can do it. There's an incredible life that awaits you.

Bethany Williams &
Vince Nelson

Chapter 1

THE LOVE SHACK

His Story...

This was a day I had dreamed about all week and had prepared for in my mind. It was my escape from the client meetings and financial portfolios I reviewed, weekend in a cabin, far away from all responsibilities with a beautiful blond bombshell to have a love affair with.

I had driven up to the cabin late Friday, woke up early Saturday, had my breakfast, cut fire wood, and was now preparing a banquet fit for a queen. Listening to the crackling fire while roasting the orange marinated salmon, new potatoes, and asparagus covered in an olive oil thyme glaze, my lips could taste it. But more than the taste of an amazing meal was the taste of my lovers lips on mine.

Making sure the fireplace had a roaring flame after adding a few more logs, I set the table, day dreaming of her arrival. Waiting to hear the tires of her car on the sandy road that lead up to the cabin, I hurried to make sure the table was set, the lights were down, and the music was playing softly in the background.

I thought back to the previous week, her eyes that pierced my soul, knowing all of me, yet still showing me honor despite all my faults.

Her blonde hair flowed, rippling like a Colorado river glistening in the sun when she laughed. Her smile was joyful and intoxicating.

This was the woman I long to passionately kiss, hold, and get lost in her eyes. This would be a night to be remembered.

In the distance I could hear the car driving slowly up the gravel road. I heard a door open and shut. She's finally here. My heart raced a hundred miles an hour. My lover had arrived.

Her story...

The garden that was in front of the cabin was beautiful. It was the first thing I saw getting out of the car, and it was dotted with roses and birds of paradise. He had spent a long time making it the perfect garden. There were flowering bushes surrounding the path, and the smell wafted past as I walked up to the cabin. I stopped, breathed deeply, and took it all in. I removed my shoes, leaving behind the vestiges of a busy work week. I could smell the comfort of burnt logs from the fire inside. Peace settled into my heart. I felt content.

I entered through the cabin door and was immediately swept into his open arms. I was passionately embraced and he kissed me, pulling me into him closer and closer. His arms wrapped around me, holding me tight. I felt fully desired, full and complete. I had the realization that I am living each day in full embrace. It is incredible. I am known and still fully loved.

Troubles seem less pressing as I walk through life hand in hand with this amazing man. How is this possible? He knows my weaknesses, my past failures, and all I've done wrong and he still loves me. He accepts me. He knows me yet somehow still sees me and accepts me for who I am. He adores me. Looking back to that day, I recall the feeling of romance so vividly. I recall my thoughts and emotions with clarity.

I have been waiting all day for this.

Swept into open arms, we fall into a plushy chair as he wraps his arms around me and we embrace, long and slow. Time stands still for several moments. I can hear his breaths as they exhale from the chest that is pressed up against me. I can feel his breath on my neck. The energy flows freely from his body to mine. He is excited to see me. I can feel his desire. I can feel a magnetic attraction pulling us together. His kisses brush against my lips again and again. He presses into me, burrowing deeper and deeper as his mouth explores my mouth with a passion and a hunger for more. His desire is palpable. It is like a drug—once tasted—I cannot imagine living without it- without him.

I wish that this one moment could last a lifetime. I look deep into his eyes and the gaze lasts for several moments. I know what is coming next, we will join as one. I am living in acceptance and love—a place where there's no games and no drama. It's a place of deep peace and vulnerability where it's truly safe to be me. I long to reveal myself to him, to reveal all of me.

Before the next kiss it hits me, how is this possible? It feels daring and dangerous, yet it is safe and secure. How is it possible we've been married for years, yet it gets better and better with each passing moment?

Let us invite you on the journey that leads to this sacred place. We will start at the beginning.

Chapter 1 Reflections—The Love Shack

- For Singles: What do your relational dreams look like?
  - When you grab your favorite beverage and sit relaxing on the couch, and you reflect, what does life look like with the man/woman you are dreaming of?
  - What do they like to do?
  - What is important to you about them?
- For Marrieds: What originally attracted you to your mate?
  - What was it about them that you really loved and desired?
  - What type of activities did you dream about doing together?
- Have you stopped dreaming about what can be? And if so, why?

Chapter 2

"HECK NO!": DEALING WITH STEREOTYPES AND THE OUTER IMAGE

I had decided at this point of my life that I had a "broken picker," and this wasn't just from my own thoughts, but actually my counselor had introduced me to this phrase and concept. Because of this revelation, the call from Tammy Kling that said she had someone I should meet left me perplexed. I had met Tammy the day I did my TEDx talk. She was a fellow speaker. We immediately connected. She said he was an ex-pastor working at Fidelity Investments. I thought, "Oh, heck no." I envisioned an overly critical, religious to a fault highly legalistic man. She said he was divorced. Now, I've never pictured myself as the saintly type and I certainly couldn't picture myself with a former pastor. I did trust Tammy, so I said, "Okay, I'll meet him." I figured with my track record, I could handle one bad date.

With all the experience I'd gained in sales for profiling people in a way that would make the FBI proud, I friend requested Vince on Facebook and reviewed his profile. I had the sneaking suspicion that his profile picture was twenty years old. There were mostly motivational quotes, and I wondered why there was no actual personal content or posts. I couldn't really "see" who he was. He was cute, looked to be outdoorsy and muscular through the shoulders. He had dark hair, and I thought he was handsome. The men that I was dating at the time, post-divorce, were young and had minimal substance. I was bored.

"Don't date!" were the words of Tammy Kling, my executive coach who I found on Facebook. I was trying to get my life back together after making a train wreck of my life. "No problem" I was quick to say, not only because of the pain I caused in my past marriage, but realizing I still had a lot of healing yet to do. On top of that, I was helping lead the single ministry at Gateway Church in Southlake, Texas and was asked not to date while I was in that role, which I was more than happy to oblige. So, when Tammy called three weeks later and said "I have someone that I want you to meet," I told her "I thought you said don't date?"

She wouldn't tell me who the person was yet, but I had a pretty good idea when a gorgeous woman friend requested me on Facebook. I could tell this wasn't your normal friend request from a young gold digger gal, not that I had any money. This friend request was from a super glossy, high powered executive, international speaker, and best-selling author of six books. "Ah-ha!" I thought to myself. I bet this is who Tammy was suggesting I meet. While I was intrigued by her, I couldn't help but think "here's another materialistic, money hungry person that's probably pretty shallow." But my track record on dating was pretty awful after the divorce and I trusted Tammy, so I thought "let's give it a try."

We exchanged numbers and began to talk on the phone. He was smart, warm hearted, and easy to talk to. Due to kids and schedules, we would end up speaking very late at night.

These conversations went on for weeks. They would go from light-hearted and weather related to the deepest darkest thoughts hiding in our hearts. They traversed topics and categories. We covered everything from world hunger to the meaning of life. We talked about the dating scene, all the game playing, the ghosting, the one-night stands, and all that made dating difficult as a second-chance single. We called ourselves second chance singles, those that had been married and were now looking for a second chance at love and life. I think we were both a little petrified of actually meeting in person. We were enjoying the conversations and didn't want to ruin it all with an actual meeting and the reality of what we might think of each other once we met. We hadn't tried to impress each other. We actually did the opposite. We had tried to scare each other off. No game playing, no stories, no fake walls to pretend to be someone we were not. Both of us wanted to get to the heart of the matter and scare each other off quickly. It was about six weeks in that Tammy invited us to her house for an event and now, the pressure was on and we would meet.

Vince brought his dad to this event, so I met Vince in person the same night I met his dad. No pressure there!

He was sweet and warm.

Vince seemed physically out of shape at first glance, which made fears from my past creep up. Would he be unhealthy and end up being someone I had to care for? Would he not be able to hike and do physically active things that I enjoyed? Fears crept up quickly and covered me in a gray mist. I overanalyzed it.

The late-night phone calls were a welcome change from the thought of dating life. Rather than have to get all dressed up, start off with a façade of being the best version of me and all the work that took, it began as a friendship. I knew better though, and having Tammy introduce us still felt like a blind date, so there was a little pressure on my side. I was quick to talk about the REAL Vince, the one that other's didn't know. Within the first two conversations, I revealed dark secrets of my recent past that had lead to my own self-sabotaging behavior, and how I finally was walking in freedom from what other's thought about me. I admitted that I had lost everything in my divorce—my home, my car, my job, any savings that I had, living daily with my boys—I'd lost everything. I told Bethany all the things you would NEVER advise anyone to share early in dating. I thought for sure, "ya…this will do it. She'll be gone in no time." I removed the illusionary mask of success and protection that I had worn my entire life and a crazy thing happened…she was still there.

The more we talked, the more I discovered that she was far from the superficial person that I had initially thought. She was beautiful. I'm not referring to physical beauty…I hadn't met her yet and didn't know what kind of Facebook filters she was using, but I mean…she was thoughtful, kind, didn't belittle me for my failures, and began sharing her own struggles, fears, and failures. In the span of six weeks over many phone conversations, this was the closest I had felt to another woman in my life time. So, when Tammy invited us to finally meet face-to-face at her house, what felt like incredible peace in my heart quickly turned to immense anxiety. "What would Bethany think of me when she sees me? How tall is she really? How tall would she be in high heels?"

I wasn't short, but I wasn't tall either at 5'7".

I used to run marathons, and work out two hours a day, but those pictures of me that she had seen on Facebook were before the divorce, prior to the toll that depression had taken on my body and soul. I was fluffy (that's being kind) and recovering from deep depression. She was now about to see the current out of shape Vince. "Would she accept me?" I wasn't sure. I did what any man would do to protect myself the first time I met her, brought my dad to hide behind.

I got there early and was hard at work, helping Tammy stuff books in bags for a charity event. Then came the knock on the door! My heart stopped. "Here we go," I thought. She walked through the door, with long flowing beautiful blond hair. She was wearing a sexy leopard skin sweater. I was checking her out from her head to toe. Then came the shoes. "NOOOO...dang it, why did she have to wear high heels!" She towered over me by a couple of inches that felt like a few thousand feet. "Oh well," I thought to myself, "I've climbed many mountains before. Let's see how this goes."

 We made it past that first introduction in person and made plans to go hiking for a day as our first date. I wasn't working at the time, I had just completed a strategic SVP role that entailed doubling the size of a company and readying it for sale. I was on time-off, trying to recover emotionally from the three acquisitions, two on opposite coasts, and from my devastating divorce after fifteen years of marriage. Vince had taken the day off for our date. I was surprised that he would leave the investment world behind and take a day off. I was used to "high powered work all the time executives" that never wanted to take time off for fear of losing revenue or a business opportunity. I was battle worn. My first husband and second husband were deceased, and I was divorced from husband #3. I was dealing with the wounds that the children had endured. I was beginning to realize that the mistakes of my past had created soul wounds, land mines that caused deep fears and made me want to go into a hole and hide. I was afraid. I was afraid to fail, afraid to try, and afraid to make an attempt at a relationship, at any relationship. I felt broken. I was lonely. I think many singles are in this same place. They have been wounded, their hearts have been broken, and it is easier to run and hide than to open up and say, "hey, come and wound me again!" I believe that many of us stay in "forever singleness" due to this overwhelming fear and lack of an ability to open up to possible pain. That same paralyzing fear covered me from head to toe as I drove to meet Vince that day.

We decided to hike at the Fort Worth Nature Center. First, we met at a Cracker Barrel, had breakfast and rode together to the nature center for our hike. He was in a rental car, so we drove my Mercedes convertible to the park for our hike. He had just been in a car accident that had totaled his car. In my opinion, he was geographically undesirable. His apartment was seventy miles from my house in Rockwall. It was an hour and a half from his place to mine. "Was it even feasible to think about dating someone that was seventy miles away, even if we made it past date 1?"

We walked and talked, hiking up and down the hills that made up the nature center. The weather was cloudy and cool. Conversation came easy. We already knew each other at this point. I thought of how many of my friends went on first dates and knew nothing about their date. I thought of how different it felt to already "know" him. It was different to mix my impressions of the "physical" Vince with the character, heart, soul, and mind that I knew him to be from weeks of conversations. I had an epiphany—*maybe our dating of today in the Facebook world is too focused on the exterior, and we rule each other out before we get to know the character, heart, soul, and mind of a person. Consider how many photo filters there are today that allow us to post illusionary pictures of ourselves, pictures where we've smoothed out every wrinkle and imperfection that makes us unique.* So, as we walked and talked, I thought of how let down I had been in relationships. I thought of how much better my life would have been had I chosen a good hearted, character rich man rather than focusing on solely the exterior image. I started to think maybe I had been doing this dating thing wrong my whole life.

I made it past the introduction at Tammy's place. "Whew, Bethany doesn't like tall men. Maybe I have a chance," I thought to myself.

It was now time to do our official date…get dressed up, drive up in my cool sports car, and play the part. Nah, that was the furthest thing from what we both experienced. As I was driving up to the Cracker Barrel we had decided to meet at, I was thinking about how I had totaled my car a week before we met and was now going on a first date in a rental car. "What a way to impress a girl!" Not only that, but we had decided to go on a hike. I liked that idea, we were dressing down and it would be relaxed, but I didn't know it would be this relaxed. Bethany was wearing sweat pants. She had a ball cap on, and wasn't wearing makeup. No pretending here. I was a little uncomfortable with getting into her red convertible Mercedes, first of all, because she was driving an expensive status symbol that I didn't have and secondly, because I wasn't driving. I was NOT in control here. This was uncomfortable, but at the same time, an interesting adventure, and I was up for the challenge.

The more we hiked and talked, the more I realized it had been years since I had done the things I loved to do like backpack, climb, kayak, and live in the great outdoors. Years of depression from my marital failures had caused me to lose sight of the things that I enjoyed, that were part of who I was. Yet, here I was, back doing the things I loved with this very intriguing woman who I could tell was determined to do the opposite of impress me. We continued our hike and were slowly getting to know each other better. The interesting thing about the date was that parts of the hike became less and less about her and the date and more a time of introspection for me. As I was beginning to like her more, I realized how I judged her when I first saw her Facebook picture. I realized my first reaction to not just women, but people, was to judge them by the stereotypes I had in my mind from my previous experiences in life. This limited not them, but me. It limited me from learning about the fascinating things about others. It limited me from wanting to reveal myself to them. It caused me to miss the depths of real friendship that grow out of acceptance, not judgement. On that hike I was beginning to throw away the measuring stick that I measured everyone by, including myself. It would no longer be about pre-judging Bethany. I was beginning a new journey for the first time in my life of getting to know someone without any preconceived ideas of her or even a desire to get something from her. This was truthful living, not illusionary dating. This was real freedom in dating, no matter if there was a second date or not.

We summited a small hill at that moment and looked out over the lake and hills below. I looked at her and was beginning to experience real intimacy for the first time in my life. This woman was beautiful. No, that's not the word. This woman was breathtaking, and I wanted to go on a journey with her. I took her hand, looked at her, drew her close, and kissed her. It was a kiss I will never forget. What made it memorable was not that it was the most passionate kiss, rather it was the first kiss I ever experienced that was about a deep emotional connection and a journey of the inward soul.

Chapter 2 Reflections—"Heck No!": Dealing with Stereotypes and the Outer Image

Maybe our dating of today in the Facebook world is too focused on the exterior, and we rule each other out before we get to know the character, heart, soul, and mind of a person.

Is *your* first reaction to people, to judge them by the stereotypes that you have in your mind from previous experiences in life? This limits not them, but you. It limits you from learning about the fascinating things about others. It limits you from wanting to reveal yourself to them. It causes you to miss the depths of real friendship that grow out of acceptance, not judgement.

- What if the limitations of how we see others and how we see ourselves, limit the amazing humans that we could find and experience love and a full life with?

- Are you judging people by stereotypes or based on your past life experiences?

- What kind of relationships are you seeking? Are you seeking heart connections or physical attraction?

- How do you see others? Do you see their heart first? Or are you clouded by their appearance, their bank balance, the car they drive, or the house or job that they possess before you get to know their heart?

- Do you believe that you could change the way that you see others by looking into their heart before evaluating them based on their circumstances and plot in life?

- ACTIVITIES: Do you/are you doing the things you enjoy? If not, why not?

Videos:

Throw Away the Measuring Stick:

http://bit.ly/throwawaythemeasuringstick

Chapter 3

TO FIND THE ONE, SAY THEY'RE "NOT THE ONE!"

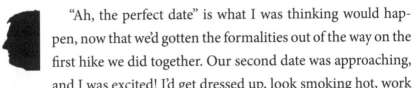"Ah, the perfect date" is what I was thinking would happen, now that we'd gotten the formalities out of the way on the first hike we did together. Our second date was approaching, and I was excited! I'd get dressed up, look smoking hot, work out a little bit to firm up my pecks and biceps, shave, shower, put my best cologne on, and pick up my hot date. Of course, she'd be all dolled up, have her best dress on, her hair perfectly styled, and wear the kind of intoxicating perfume that when I'd get close to her neck, the smell of it would make my testosterone go into overdrive. I'd be the perfect gentleman, we'd laugh over dinner, we'd share the best stories we had to offer, and the night would end in a magical way. At least that's the kind of date that was in my head. That's not how the date went.

I was tired after working a long week. I cleaned up quickly. Running errands for the kids had made me a bit behind schedule. I jumped into my Honda Civic rental car. I was still embarrassed because I didn't have my new permanent car yet. In addition to that, my credit wasn't good coming out of my divorce. I was struggling to find a new car at a price that I could afford. This didn't help my confidence. Then there was the exhaustive drive. I lived in Fort Worth, and she lived an hour and a half away in Rockwall, Texas. I was stressed because I was running late and had a very long drive ahead. I finally arrived at her house. It looked like it was in a million-dollar neighborhood. Here I was in a rental car, just having left my small apartment. I was standing at the door to what looked like a mansion. My ego felt like a balloon that someone had deflated. I knocked.

The door opened and there stood a very tall grown man with a massive beard, "Mom, your date's here" he chuckled as he invited me in. He towered over me and quickly began barraging me with questions about what I did for a living. "So, you're a financial adviser I hear, you must make a lot of cash. You can spend your extra mullah on me," Bethany's son said.

Finally, Bethany walked into the room. So far, this date wasn't going the way I had dreamed. Not only did it NOT have a big harry guy in it, but Bethany would be wearing something very different than what she had on. Sweatpants. Oh, and a tank top covered in a workout jacket. I almost forgot to mention, today she wasn't wearing any makeup either. "I'm ready," she said, as she walked out the door.

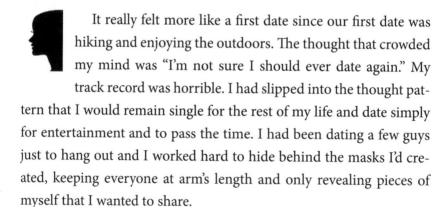 It really felt more like a first date since our first date was hiking and enjoying the outdoors. The thought that crowded my mind was "I'm not sure I should ever date again." My track record was horrible. I had slipped into the thought pattern that I would remain single for the rest of my life and date simply for entertainment and to pass the time. I had been dating a few guys just to hang out and I worked hard to hide behind the masks I'd created, keeping everyone at arm's length and only revealing pieces of myself that I wanted to share.

With Vince I thought, "Let's just get to know each other authentically and real." I figured we could develop a friendship that could last a lifetime. Anything beyond that I felt was impossible.

He arrived at the house. I certainly didn't want to drive an hour and a half for a date. In my mind if he wanted to pursue this he could drive, because it was probably a waste of our time anyways. So, he made the long drive to my house.

At this point in my life I was living with my two boys, Caleb was still in high school and Brandon, a full-grown man still enjoying the benefits of life at home. Caleb was out for the evening as he often was and Brandon answered the door. If I had been concerned with impressing Vince and not scaring him off, I probably would have cared enough to answer the door myself. I also didn't dress up or apply makeup. I had spent so many years in relationships dating where we were both pretending, that I was tired of the games and the illusions. If I wanted to be deep in an illusion, I could read a love story or watch a chick flick. In life, I was tired of playing make believe and then watching my prince turn into a frog once I married them. In my mind, he wouldn't be around long—so "whatever," I thought. I figured we wouldn't make it past date two.

In my attempts to find love in my life I had continually failed. The deep intense love I'd had with my first husband that still caused pain ended in desertion, divorce, and ultimately he died. In the rearview mirror, I saw my selfishness, my difficult self-righteous personality, and all the ways I had ruined every relationship. I had poor self-esteem, a condemning and cruel tongue, and hatred and bitterness that stemmed from losing my first love that seemed to infiltrate any relationship I developed. I didn't see myself as worthy or loveable. I couldn't imagine someone wanting to deeply love me.

A rental car pulls up and out pops Vince. I watch him from inside the house, half of me wondering why the heck I'm even trying. It's like losing $100,000 at the craps table in Vegas and continuing to play.

We got a quick bite to eat at a local hole-in-the-wall and came back to her home to talk some more. It was far from a glamorous date. It was the kind of date that was more like a couple of guys hanging out for the evening. We already had been sharing some pretty deep things about ourselves over the phone. We had determined to set aside pretension and best appearances and let the "REAL" us be seen. Let me tell you, it was raw and real. I mean, ugly real sometimes. We both shared our stories, and included all the worst parts.

Have you ever watched the movie *How to Lose A Guy in Ten Days*? Well that's what was happening. Like the woman in the movie, we shared the kind of stuff that was guaranteed to run the other off. I shared details of the affair that ruined my marriage. I shared my current insecurities. I talked about the damage the affair had caused and what I had learned about myself through it. I talked about the terrible credit I had, how I left everything to my ex-wife because of my guilt. I even talked about the old, ugly apartment I lived in that I'd never want her to see. I laid it all out. I was deeply vulnerable, and I was certain that this would be the last date. So, I kissed her goodnight and drove back home thinking "Yup, that did it. She won't date me again. Who would want a guy that was my age, that had lost everything, was starting over and was insecure about where he was in life?"

Despite all of this, I felt free. I didn't have to pretend I was someone that I wasn't. I was me, the real me, and it felt good. I wasn't spending lots of emotional energy trying to impress her. At this point in my life, I wasn't interested in dating someone that I'd have to impress. I was done with that after the affair and the lies that I'd told to create an illusion for my ex-wife that everything was okay and with the lies I'd told to the woman that I had an affair with that all would work out well in the end. I was done pretending. That was a prison I would never go back to. If a woman wasn't going to accept me for just plain ordinary me, then I wasn't interested.

 We decided to grab some food and eat at the house. He was incredibly transparent and real. I revealed pieces of my past that would have caused a hedonistic sinner to blush, yet Vince didn't even blink. This shocked me. He was a former pastor and I expected him to "you should, you shouldn't have" me. I expected extreme judgement and distaste for the decisions of my past. But the impossible seemed to be happening. He didn't judge me. He was accepting and real. We focused on each other's hearts and the deep crevices of our soul wounds and the deep feelings of hurt that surrounded our hearts. We talked openly about failures. He talked about the catastrophe that led to the ending of his marriage.

I had been cheated on, yet instead of rage, I felt compassion for him. I had experienced every kind of hurt in relationships: physical abuse, verbal abuse, and betrayal. But rather than see him as an abuser and applying my past relational fears and hatred to him, I saw his heart and it was renewed.

All I'd wanted all my life was for someone to be this vulnerable and this real. I had never found transparency this raw and real and it felt comforting. I could see past the external and straight into his heart. He was a new man. He was not the man that had created devastation in his marriage and life. He was a man renewed. He was forgiving and kind. He was non-judgmental and thoughtful. He was genuine. Rather than talk about his ex-wife and all her failures, his conversation focused on what he'd done wrong, what he'd learned, and how he would walk differently going forward having learned these painful lessons. I had learned through my own marriages that it is never one-sided. Two people fail in a marriage. Yet he didn't focus on any of her failures; his conversation focused solely on what he had learned from his failures. I can honestly say I have never experienced such transparency. As we sat and talked, I felt a hunger to know him more. We were not focused on the physical, but instead we were getting to know each other's hearts. It took a lot of the pressure off. I found him handsome, but that was not my focus. Handsome devils had caused me intense pain in life, and I had pursued physical specimens seeking out perfect bodies just to be devastated by dark hearts. I was definitely up for another date and I was starting to think "Hmmm, where is this going to go?"

There was a third date! I couldn't believe it. She actually talked to me the next day and didn't blow me off. She wanted to see me again. I knew she was dating other guys, but she still wanted to see me. Half of me wanted to see her again because I was attracted to her and the other half wanted to prove that she'd be the first to bail as I shared more details about my unflattering life.

I wasn't quite ready for the no makeup and sweat pant dates at first, but a funny thing happened over time. We were at ease. There was no sense of nervousness or anxiety. There was no manipulation of the conversation, on either end. She shared deep things about her own insecurities and failures as I shared mine.

I could tell she was doing the same thing to me that I was to her, seeing who could one-up the other with worse character flaws, failures in our marriages, and things we had done that would cause most people to end the date and never return a text. There were moments she shared deep painful experiences and poor choices she had made. She was revealing some of the deepest places she had been hurt before by others. She'd share about her failures in her marriages, both of her husbands had died. Then, she shared about the failures of her third marriage.

As she revealed those deep wounds, I could see her almost wince, waiting for me to say condemning words like "that's really screwed up" or "dang, you've really messed up a lot of marriages." But how could I say anything like that? I had been a terrible failure towards my ex-wife, to my kids, to the people I led in church, but most of all to myself and God. I had no place to judge her. As she shared deeply vulnerable things about her life, my heart went out to her. I wanted her to experience the same forgiveness of self and healing that I was experiencing having learned painful lessons from my own failures. As we both shared deeper and deeper things about our own failures and learnings, there was a sense of comfort, safety, and healing that was happening between us.

Date three, lead to date five, ten, and we began to lose count. I saw in Bethany something that was beautiful beyond words and so priceless. In the early dating days, many times she said to me, "Vince, why would you want to date someone who's been married so many times? I wouldn't blame you if you never called me again." My reply to her the first time, the third time, and the tenth was always the same, "Bethany, when you talk about your past marriages, you don't talk about how your husbands' screwed up. You talk about your own failures in marriage. You take ownership of the areas you screwed up in, and you learn from that. You have one of the most important attributes I would want the person I date to have…a receptive heart. A heart that learns and grows."

One of the most endearing qualities is a capable and transparent woman, like the one in Proverbs 31. I began to discover a lot of traits I loved about her.

 The hardest thing I had to overcome was to realize that a lifetime of bad decisions had left me uncomfortable in a healthy relationship. I felt awkward. I was familiar with abuse in all its forms and a part of me deep inside felt that abuse is all that I was worthy of. I kept thinking and saying to Vince, "you need a sweet church lady, Vince, not someone like me;" or "you are way too good for me." I knew he wanted to write a book and speak and I feared that my past and the decisions I'd made could keep him from being selected to speak at certain faith-based organizations. I didn't want to hold him back and I feared that he could not possibly comprehend the judgement others would weigh on him because of me.

I felt like a commoner trying to date a nobleman. Now, all these feelings were crowding in despite the knowledge of what had happened to him in his life. Often feelings are not rational, but they are real to the person experiencing them. I saw a man who had pastored thousands and I felt like the woman at the well in the Bible. I could hear Jesus' words "You're right! You don't have a husband—for you have had five husbands, and you aren't even married to the man you're living with now" (John 4:17-18 NLT).

I actually felt comfortable in abusive relationships. I thought, "Hmmm, how do you un-train yourself from unhealthy relationships?" I figured it was probably like eating right and exercising; I was going to have to take it one step, one day at a time with a slow evolution to a new reality. I found myself continually wanting to slide back into abuse. It was my comfort zone. I'd never heard anyone talk about an abuse accepting mindset, so I thought maybe it was only me and I was crazy. It felt so uncomfortable to be treated with love and respect. I began to realize that I was to blame for accepting the men in my life. I hadn't valued myself.

I had let my poor self-esteem sink me into accepting "less-than" relationships that didn't require total intimacy or complete emotional investment on my part. I looked around and quickly realized that I was not in the minority. Women all around me were doing the same thing.

But when the pain of change is less than the pain of staying the same, you become motivated to change! For some people it's the only escape from a life of bad choices and negative patterns in relationships.

I decided I had to re-train my brain. I decided to try desperately to accept the value God said I had. It was difficult. It was like hiking up a mountain against a strong, fifty mile an hour wind.

The only thing that kept me going was the constant reminder of how poorly my past decisions had turned out. They say "if you do what you always have done, you will get what you always have gotten." It was time to go after something new. Let's face it, I had nothing to lose and everything to gain. So, the truth and love journey began as our story was just beginning.

 If we started dating by playing games with each other and hiding, I never would have seen this incredibly receptive heart she possessed that wanted to learn from her mistakes.

I saw it was the fuel for her to live truthfully with herself and others. That receptivity was the same fuel that allowed me to be honest with myself and not duck and cover in relationships.

Was it painful to take off the mask? Heck yes, but having tasted the freedom of learning to love and accept myself as a valuable person, I never wanted to go back to living an illusion that forever would isolate me and make me lonely. I was learning I was worthy of being loved, I was lovable, and learning how to love others.

Wearing masks in relationships and hiding our feelings for fear of being rejected is an illusionary prison. Illusionary living promises to protect your heart—but forever keeps you in a prison where you will starve for the intimate affection of others. But this intimate affection is what your soul is designed to experience.

Could this relationship that began between Bethany and me have ended quickly by being transparent and gut-level honest? Sure, it could, but in our minds if it did, it wasn't something we really wanted. We both were in a similar place in life where we were tired of playing games with people. We were both ready to be the real us, no matter if the other person received us or not.

In that place of realness, the soil of life was being cultivated for a healthy relationship to emerge. Ugly truth shared, mixed with awareness of our own flawed hearts that longed to be loved, created a safe place to be vulnerable with each other. Truth with love and understanding of the other led to vulnerability which lead to intimacy and there it is—the most coveted prize we see in the rarest of desirable relationships—intimacy, a place where you are fully known, know the other fully, and are still embraced, faults and all.

Chapter 3 Reflections- "Heck No!": To Find the One Say They are Not the One

- Do you convince yourself that each guy or gal that you date is definitely going to be the one? Can you work on convincing yourself that each one is not the one and allow time to explore the relationship? It will put less pressure on the relationship and allow things to develop.

- Do you fall into game playing? Maybe it has snuck in without you even noticing it.

Let's also reflect these two relational issues of the heart.

Receptive heart: When you or your date/mate talk about your past, do you talk about how your past relationships screwed up or do talk about your own failures? Do you take ownership of the areas you screwed up in, and have you learned from them? Are you developing one of the most important attributes anyone would want in the person they'd want to date—a receptive heart? Are you developing a heart that listens, learns, and grows?

Comfortable in abuse: Do you feel comfortable in abusive relationships? If yes, can you commit to taking it one step, one day at a time with a slow evolution to a new reality? Do you find yourself continually wanting to slide back into abuse? Could it possibly be your comfort zone.? Do you believe that you may have an abuse-accepting mindset? Does it feel uncomfortable to be treated with love and respect?

If you are beginning to identify your abuse comfort thinking and actions, continue reading and we will cover this in more detail as we progress through the chapters of this book. We also encourage you to read Vince's book, *Child of the King,* to learn how to receive and live the incredible value that you already have.

To order it online, type the following web address:

http://bit.ly/Childofthekingbook

Chapter 4

AUTHENTICITY CREATES ATTRACTION

My experience with truth had, up to this point, resulted in rejection, fights, or pain. It was to me a bit of like putting my hand on a hot stove. I had erred so many times in relationships that I decided that there was no other option other than to follow a different path. I decided to follow the path of extreme truth. The journey had a frightfully difficult start. As a single again individual, I was trying to date with integrity and honesty. I began telling the prospective men exactly why I had chosen to date them or not to date as the case may be. As I ventured into this truth journey, it was not well received. I recognized very quickly that the truth was painful to most, if not to all of us. I guess that is why so many people develop a habit in their lives of telling white lies. I rejected the white lies and ventured forth with this concept of an absolute truth journey. Ouch! Each time I would try this approach it was met with anger and a debate. Apparently, when faced with the harsh truth, many thought they could argue me out of the information that I had shared. Let's take my take with Pete, for example. He was very young, about the age of my youngest son. I told him that I wasn't attracted to him, and he argued that he was attractive. I tried to explain that it wasn't that he wasn't handsome, it was that he was not attractive to me. There was no chemistry. It ended in an argument. Then there was Bill. Bill had lied about his age on Match.com. He was ten years older than he had stated, and I didn't feel a connection due to our age difference. I told him that I didn't want to date an older guy, and he argued with me that he was young in his thinking and activities. He wanted to prove to me that he was datable. I asked him why he lied about his age and he got defensive. I wasn't interested in dating him, and the truth did not set well with him.

I met Greg, and we dated. I discovered very quickly that his personality wasn't a match to mine. When I told him that, he argued that we were a perfect match. It was all very strange to me. I felt that if my value was given to me from my Creator, then surely I could be honest and be able to find someone eventually who would honor that approach.

I watched from afar as the friends around me ventured in and out of dating and I watched the games that they would play. They danced in illusion and shook hands with lies. I craved intimacy.

When I was a teenager I had fallen in love, deeply in love. We had a share everything, honest relationship that formed a tight bond of love. I had never experienced a bond like this that was open and vulnerable. I felt loved, secure, and at peace. We were young, and after eight years he abandoned me. We continued to be friends as he journeyed down a dark path of drug addiction. It was a path that I had chosen not to live for my daughter and I. We continued to talk weekly, and he was my best friend. Despite living apart, he knew me like no other and our rich conversations were a lifeline to me during this time in my life.

Jeff died in a motorcycle accident when my oldest daughter was eight years old. It was a traumatic part of my past that I had never been able to let go of. Since his death, I have never experienced that kind of bond and part of me wondered if I ever would again.

Meeting Vince had given me hope.

We started down the road to complete truth. He didn't argue with me about the truth. He didn't tell me I was wrong. He accepted the stark truth as truth. The pure authenticity and honesty that we shared began to create an intense attraction. I began to recognize that authenticity creates attraction.

This was a revolutionary thought at this point in my life. I had spent most of my life running from authenticity and the truth and chasing after physical attraction and illusion. It was a complicated thought, what if attraction was found in pure authenticity and could be found in many different people, shapes, sizes and personalities. What if we are all running after the wrong goal and missing the GOLD hidden in people everywhere? In truth, if this is the case, there are gems of guys and gals everywhere that would match to the single adults that are searching, if only they knew the formula and could start this journey.

I thought deeply about authenticity creating attraction and several relationships came to mind. I watched a "60 Minutes" from Australia on a friend of Tammy's named Nick Vujicic. This man with no arms and no legs is happily married with four children. His wife, Kanae, couldn't have made his physical appearance her primary focus when dating. Their relationship sparks with love. I also have followed Joni Erickson Tada, the quadriplegic who paints with her mouth. She had a swimming accident as a teenager, leaving her paralyzed from the shoulders down. I noticed that she was happily married and I devoured the book of her love affair with her husband. She has written over forty books, paints with her teeth and is an advocate for people with disabilities. I bet her husband Ken didn't focus primarily on her physical appearance. These stories began to sink into my heart and soul as I realized that the Facebook world I lived in had been stealing my ability to see the hearts and souls of the people around me.

What if we are all running after the wrong goal and missing the GOLD hidden in people everywhere? It was such an unbelievable reality.

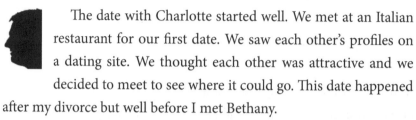 The date with Charlotte started well. We met at an Italian restaurant for our first date. We saw each other's profiles on a dating site. We thought each other was attractive and we decided to meet to see where it could go. This date happened after my divorce but well before I met Bethany.

I was in the process of rebuilding my life and social network of friends after my affair. I was really raw emotionally, trying to rediscover if I was the leader I had been prior to the affair. I had lived in a prison of isolation for decades of my life for fear of being hurt and rejected. I had never revealed the "real me" with my thoughts and feelings. For me, hiding was a normal place to be. Looking back, I saw that as I hid who I was, I was trying to figure out what others thought about me and trying to present that person I thought they wanted. How exhausting that was! I was a different person now. I had finally learned how to accept all of me as a valuable person, faults and all. So, I was determined going forward that I would be honest about who I was, no matter the cost.

Charlotte was sharing about her job, her Instagram posts, and how she was enjoying the weather. In my mind all I heard was "job blah blah blah, Instagram blah blah, weather blah blah blah." I wanted a real conversation. I had a heart that had been parched in a dessert of shallow relationships. So I dived in, "The weather has been fantastic. It's perfect hiking weather. I love adventures. You know my life has been an adventure. After being a pastor for seventeen years and having an affair, I'm learning how to be healthy again and really live." I've never seen a woman run faster from me than Charlotte. In a matter of five minutes the date was over, and I never heard from Charlotte again.

I was learning how to date again. I was experiencing rejection after rejection. I apparently was too raw and too real. One lady told me I wasn't manly enough for her. It felt like she didn't like men who were honest with their emotional feelings and vulnerabilities. I was very confused on the dating scene.

So you would think I just gave up, right? Or at least went back to my familiar place of hiding my heart. Isn't that why so many of us put the mask back on, for fear of continually being hurt and rejected? In my past, that would have been exactly where I would have retreated to, but not this time. I've since discovered that sometimes what seems like loss is actually a win. I know I dodged a bullet several times.

Having been finally freed from the energy draining efforts of trying to please others because I didn't accept myself, I was determined to be the real me, regardless of what other's thought. I also was hungry to find the very thing I was finally willing to be, real. I wanted a woman who was courageous enough to be vulnerable and reveal the beauty of her true self, faults and all, and in walked Bethany into my life.

 One of the shocking realities I discovered was an interesting world of opposites. Each time I would share a deep emotional weakness or fear with Vince, I'd expect him to run for the hills. The result was a complete opposite to what I had expected. We would be closer at the outset of my sharing. We would both feel peace and security. The information that I expected to send him into shock factor would bring us closer together and further cement our bond. We tried this several times, each time sharing a deep betrayal from our past, fully expected to break up. The truth was harsh.

We would share the truth and wait for the backlash. What we had done in our pasts was not pretty. We would spend weeks bolstering up our nerve to share something with each other that we felt would end our relationship, and the opposite happened. We became deeply connected, deeply intimate and it was forming a deep love and connection that we never expected to occur. A part of me felt shock. How could I have gone my whole life not realizing this truth? Was this the stuff that created lifelong bonds and relationships that lasted 30, 40, 50, or even 60 years or longer? How had I gone so many years without understanding how to create an intimate and long-standing relationship? I realized that there was nowhere in my life up to this point that this information had been shared.

There was not a "how-to book" on intimacy. There was no answer book that allowed someone to seek the answers and find solutions to the deepest of dilemmas. How do you create an intimate relationship that lasts the test of time? I felt that I was a discoverer. I may not be discovering the Americas like Christopher Columbus, but I was on a journey of discovery of my own. It wasn't too late. I was researching the deep heart of man and how to connect to another human being from the deepest parts of their heart and soul. I was learning how to accept my value from my Creator and not live in fear of being rejected, deserted, and alone. I was striking out to fully know another human being and to love him unconditionally, accepting all that God had created in him.

And as a result I was experiencing deep freedom. I was free from the fear that had surrounded me for a lifetime. I was free from the burden of making things happen in relationships and trying to control my mate. I was suddenly free to accept the path God had before me, to trust him fully and completely and let come what may. I needed to accept that God was my maker and that he could meet my needs. Joy came from God, not my mate. As I began to fully understand where joy came from, and where my acceptance, happiness, and love came from, I began to release the demands from the man that I was dating. He didn't have to make me happy. He didn't have to complete me.

He didn't have to do what I said. I didn't have to check his Facebook page, try to figure out where he was, and stalk his locations. I could rest and relax, and know that God was my provider, my supplier of joy and happiness. I could rest in His amazing arms and let Him give me a helpmate to go through life with. I didn't need someone to do anything other than be the incredible person that God made them to be, and together we could go through life on an adventure together. It freed me to stop striving. It put my heart at rest. It was from this place that Vince and I began our relationship together. Rest. Receive. Trust. Walking in faith, our relationship began to blossom.

Are there areas of your life that you need to give to God?

Water to my soul. This was the first time I ever had a re-lationship like this with anyone and it was freeing. It was peaceful, it was life-giving and nurturing, and at the same time it challenged me to let go of the past fears and failures that held me back from being the real me. It also did something else. It was freeing me to live my purpose. We discussed openly about what our purpose was and what we wanted to accomplish in life. We were now at the age where we were beginning to think about legacy and the difference we wanted to make.

Rather than being fearful that perhaps what I feel passionate about doing is something she wouldn't like, I shared about my heart to men-tor men and help people. I found as I shared, she shared and we dis-covered our purposes were uniquely aligned to help others. Because I had no preconceived idea that Bethany had to make me whole or meet my needs, I could be completely transparent with my thoughts and desires. I shared who I was and for the first time found someone who not only wanted to go on the truth journey with me because that's where she was at, I discovered a person who I could do life with, climb mountains with, write and be creative with.

I was almost half a century old and this was the first time in my life that I was learning the power of deep vulnerability and connection of the human soul. No one in all my years of even being a pastor ever taught me how to experience incredible relationships. Was it because so many of us walk around with masks on for fear of being hurt? I still wonder that today.

I grew up as an American male. Our culture teaches little boys to be tough, don't cry, toughen up when you get your feelings hurt, don't wear your emotions on your sleeves. We're taught to stuff, hide, and duck and cover. The strength of a man is in being a steady rock that others can depend on, at least that's what I learned growing up. Perhaps we've gotten it wrong though. Perhaps the strength of character the world so desperately needs is a man or woman who finds the courage to receive love, and to learn how to accept their self when they fail. Maybe it's the man or woman who finds the courage and true strength to reach out to people and be real. And just maybe there will be that time when your own authenticity gives another person the courage to be real and finally be free from the prison that has kept them from being their true magnificent selves.

With Bethany, I was just beginning to learn authenticity was very attractive. Being vulnerable creates authenticity, and vulnerability is what creates intimacy. Bethany and I were learning that being vulnerable is like climbing a mountain. Sometimes you come to a ledge that you have to climb over and you can see a thousand feet down. Like climbing, we were learning that our relationship could be scary because you could be rejected by others. Having climbed many mountains before, let us tell you, the summit of deep intimacy is worth the journey.

Chapter 4 Reflections—Authenticity Creates Attraction

What if attraction is found in pure authenticity and could be found in many different people, shapes, sizes and personalities? What if we are all running after the wrong goal and missing the GOLD hidden in people everywhere? In truth, if this is the case, there are gems of guys and gals everywhere that would match the single adults that are searching, if only they knew the formula and could start this journey. It is such an unbelievable reality.

If you can rest in who you are and stop trying to please others, you can be the real you, regardless of what others think. Be courageous enough to be vulnerable and reveal the beauty of your true self, faults and all. This is where real life is found. This is the nourishing soil that cultivates great relationships.

Perhaps the strength of character the world so desperately needs is a man or woman who finds the courage to receive love, and to learn how to accept their value, despite their failures. In this place, there is no need to be someone you are not. It's a place of rest and acceptance. It's also the place where you can love others just as they are. When you're on this path, there will be a time when your own authenticity gives another person the courage to be real and finally be free from the prison that has kept them from being their true magnificent selves. Your authenticity will spark authenticity in others.

- Do you wear a mask? If so, what does it look like? Do the filters you put on your Facebook profile filter into real life?

- What does the real you look like behind the mask? Do the people in your life know the real you?

- Have you forgotten who you really are and the activities in life you enjoy?

- What will it take for you to lay down your mask and reveal the real you?

Chapter 5

THE START OF THE
INWARD JOURNEY

My phone vibrated with a new text. It was from Vince. It said that he wouldn't be texting me today, he was dealing with some emotional weight. I loved the honesty we were sharing. We had decided not to ghost each other, but to inform the other one if we decided to take a break from communication. Last night he had called to apologize, he felt that he had reacted to me in a way that he thought could have been handled better. I didn't even know what he was talking about. The thought that he was thinking through how he treated me and looking at ways to treat me better was an astounding thought and a reality that I had never faced before despite numerous previous relationships and having been married before.

I felt peace and security in our relationship. Even though we had just started dating, I felt that I knew him better than I had ever known anyone. We hadn't revealed our newfound dating relationship to our kids; I'm not sure what they would think. The truth journey that we both thought initially sounded very crazy was creating an intense security. I felt that I could be myself. I was revealing my true feelings without worrying about retribution. He wasn't using what I shared against me. He wasn't attacking me verbally. We were exploring the land mines of wounds from our past relationships and our childhoods and beginning to learn how to avoid causing each other pain accidentally by stepping on a past wound.

Vince was writing a book about his failures and the ability to let go of the shame that often keeps us in prisons. One day he mentioned the meaning of the word *intimacy* and it really surprised me. I am constantly set aback with all my education and background when I encounter a new, very important, fact of life that I should have known by now. He defined intimacy as "To be fully known, know the other person fully, and to be completely embraced." I remember thinking "sign me up!" He believed that it truly meant no measuring, no shame, and fully embracing that person where they were in life. Wow, can you imagine what life would be like if your friends and family accepted you like that?

We decided that was our new goal. We wanted to not only love each other that way, but we wanted to truly love our friends, family, and children that way. We wanted to fully know them and fully accept them, and have them feel our full embrace. What could possibly be better than that?

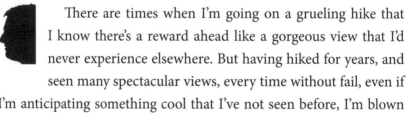

There are times when I'm going on a grueling hike that I know there's a reward ahead like a gorgeous view that I'd never experience elsewhere. But having hiked for years, and seen many spectacular views, every time without fail, even if I'm anticipating something cool that I've not seen before, I'm blown away when I arrive at the breathtaking view before me. When I've been climbing for hours, and I'm hot, sweaty, and dirty, and I come around the corner of a mountain and see a spectacular valley below, then at that moment a cool breeze refreshes my soul. I can breathe. I feel peace. I can finally rest and take it all in.

Living life up to this point with relationships was that mountain I was climbing and the corner I just turned led me into this life-changing place with Bethany and the relational journey that we were on.

I was experiencing something that I knew existed, but I had never experienced in my four plus decades of living, deep, life giving intimacy. I can't say I was brilliant enough to have purposefully mapped out my course in life to experience this. Honestly, I felt like I just fell into it. But looking back, I had been on a journey of the inward soul of learning how to forgive myself for the affair I had and learning how to love myself despite searing childhood trauma. It was on this personal inward journey that I was beginning to see the incredible value in me that my Creator said I had. I had read in the Bible where we are made in God's image, but I never fully understood it until now.

It wasn't about proving that I mattered to someone or even myself. That's what I thought for decades and it infected every decision and action I made. I was now in a place of no measurements.

I was priceless not because of anything I had said, done, or hadn't done. In truth trying to measure my worth, as so many of us do, was a crazy maker. Measuring always brought up the question, how much is enough? Where is the end of the measuring stick that I can finally reach? Let me tell you, in forty years of trying to be good enough and living as a perfectionist, I never found the end to that measuring stick. It wasn't until I finally realized I could never measure up and threw away the stick that I saw my value would never come from performance. The only way to live from that place was acceptance. Acceptance that I was made in God's image. God's image is immeasurable.

He's priceless. I'm made in His image; therefore, I'm priceless. I was finally coming to not only understand this but to finally receive and believe it.

Bethany and I were hiking in the Himalayas of Nepal and there was a powerful word we learned, *Namaste*. It's an amazing word that the

Nepalese really believe and live. The basic meaning is that "I see and honor the value in you given by your Creator." They not only receive that for themselves, but because of receiving it, they extend love and honor to others in the same way.

I was seeing myself and others around me, in a new way. My world view was changing, evolving, and becoming totally new and different. You would think that being a pastor for seventeen years, I would have been loving towards others and grace-filled towards myself. But I wasn't. I totally missed that our Creator's heart wasn't for us to measure, rather we are meant to walk in the truth that our value comes from Him. I've learned it's so important because to experience intimacy, something our human souls are designed to have daily, we have to be in a place where it's safe to be vulnerable and honest.

We can be in that place when we receive love, we know we have great value, and therefore can just rest and be ourselves, regardless of what others think of us. In that truth we grow secure in our self-worth and aren't phased nearly as much when we are honest with someone, but they reject us. We start to see that their rejection may not have been about us, rather that rejection came from something they are dealing with in their own life. When I come to that place of acceptance, I am now free to be me, to no longer hide, and just love others the same way.

I was beginning to understand what the Garden of Eden was really all about. In the story of Eden, we learn that before Adam and Eve ate from the Tree of the Knowledge of Good and Evil, they were completely naked and felt no shame. They were completely vulnerable and didn't judge or measure each other. They weren't criticizing what they saw in the other person, rather they just appreciated who the other person was. And they didn't feel shame themselves when they were naked. They didn't feel judged or feel like they would be rejected. They were at peace. It was in this place that they experienced deep intimacy. It wasn't until after they had eaten from that same tree that God went looking for them because they were hiding from God. They felt shame. For the first time in their lives they began measuring everything. God's first words to Adam were "where are you?" Then, when he found Adam and Eve he asked "why are you hiding?" To which Adam replied "we're naked." And God's response was "who told you, you were naked? Who told you that was bad?"

Why are you measuring yourself, Adam? Why are you pulling back from being vulnerable with me, Adam? God's pursuit of Adam and Eve was because he longed to be intimate with them. He longed for them to be intimate with each other. It was about deep connection. It was about relationship.

When I met Bethany, I was in a different place. I knew I could be honest with her even if she rejected me. And if she did reject me it might hurt, but it didn't mean I was unlovable. It would mean that maybe she wasn't the one for me. But something different happened with her. When I was vulnerable with my thoughts and feelings, Bethany listened. She didn't judge me for the affair. She was understanding when I told her I was struggling emotionally. It was safe to share with her. It was like being in Eden. I could be me. This led my heart to want to create a safe place for her. Her feelings mattered to me. I hadn't known her long, but I valued her. I saw how beautiful she was as a human being on the inside, and I wanted to love her with understanding. This was becoming the most unbelievable life-giving relationship I had ever experienced. I had turned the corner of the mountain and saw the most breathtaking view I'd ever seen, Bethany! She was a woman I could be completely me with. She allowed me to see every part of her soul, and we both found we still embraced each other, despite all the failures we'd had in our lives.

Chapter 5 Reflections—The Start of the Inward Journey

Intimacy *means "To be fully known, know the other person fully, and to be completely embraced." It means no measuring, no shame, and fully embracing that person where they are in life. Your goal is to accept your friends and family like that. The beginning of your journey is to truly love your friends, family, and children that way. Strive to fully know them and fully accept them, and have them feel your full embrace. Imagine what your life will look like when you do this.*

- Our question for you: do you value yourself? We're not speaking from a narcissistic, materialistic, or self-centered way. The question is, do you know you're valuable, even if you've messed up? Do you know that you are priceless, just the way you are, even when you are rejected for sharing your inner thoughts, emotions and failures?

- If you struggle with being vulnerable, ask yourself why. What is it that keeps you from revealing your true self? Truly think on this. Is it because someone rejected you in the past? Have you been rejected by a boyfriend, girlfriend, spouse, or even a parent? If you are struggling because of this, we invite you to read Vince's book, *Child of the King,* that will help you on your own personal journey of learning how to embrace the truth that you are priceless, just the way you are.

- In the Bible, Jesus teaches "Love your neighbor as yourself" (Matthew 22:39 NIV). Often, we do exactly that. We do love others the way we love ourselves. If we don't value ourselves in a healthy way, we don't know how to love, accept, and encourage others in a healthy way. If we measure our own failures, we'll measure other people's failures the same way. Without even realizing it, we think they aren't valuable if they don't do certain things.

- Do you value others around you? Do you create a safe place for them to be vulnerable with you? Do you allow them to share their thoughts and feelings without rejecting them with your words or with the facial reactions that you have? Do you allow them to share their failures without judging them? True intimacy involves listening and showing that you care.

A few thoughts for you to reflect on:

- Value yourself and you'll value others.

- Forgive yourself and you'll forgive others.

- Treat yourself kindly and you'll treat others with kindness.

- Embrace the value in yourself and you'll truly begin embracing others in a new way and giving them life.

Chapter 6

THE BIG REVEAL

Despite the mountaintop experience that surrounded my developing relationship with Vince, I still had the overwhelming reality of having three adult children with thoughts and feelings of their own. Not only had we not added a relationship status on Facebook or come out to any of our friends that we were technically dating but we also hadn't shared it with any of our children. Vince was at an advantage because he had met two of my three children. I hadn't met either of Vince's sons and this was a cause of great concern for me. Could I really consider dating someone whose children I had never met. Vince had one son who was 14 years old and his autistic son was 16 years old. My children were 16, 20, and 28. Neither of us had met the other's ex-spouses, nor were we anxious to.

We knew that managing through the emotions and realities with our children was going to be quite the challenge. Would they accept that we were dating? Would they accept the person that we had decided to date?

We started with the easiest thing possible. We changed our status on Facebook to dating. My twenty-year-old son was the first to respond. He said, " Oh you are really serious, I thought you were just leading him on." My youngest son thought that I was just trying to fill the vacancy left from his dad and I divorcing. My daughter was rejecting any and all recognition that I might ever date again. I completely understood her perspective. My record was pretty poor. If I were her, I wouldn't want me to ever date again either.

We did the only thing that we knew how to do in this very complicated and complex situation. We decided to pray. We did not know how this was going to go.

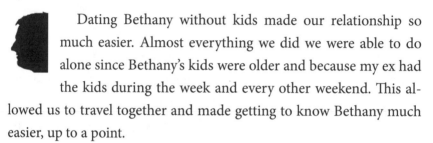 Dating Bethany without kids made our relationship so much easier. Almost everything we did we were able to do alone since Bethany's kids were older and because my ex had the kids during the week and every other weekend. This allowed us to travel together and made getting to know Bethany much easier, up to a point.

We had decided from the beginning to share everything we were thinking and feeling. We were done with game playing and that meant being vulnerable with what was going on inside our thoughts. For me, I could tell Bethany's kids weren't interested in another guy coming into their lives. I was beginning to wonder if Bethany and I were to have a long-term relationship, would work out? There were also other fears I had, fears that I was beginning to see Bethany struggle with. But because we had both determined to not live an illusionary life where we made up situations that weren't real, we would instead deal with life in its sometimes ugly and messy situations. That meant being honest with each other even when it hurt...and share our feelings we did.

She hadn't met my kids yet and for good reason. First, my youngest at the time was adamant I shouldn't date. He was so strong in his conviction that he told me if I did date and possibly marry Bethany, he would never be part of my life with her. Ouch! Then there was my ex-wife, who was just about as adamant about our kids not meeting

Bethany and wouldn't allow my older son, who has autism, to meet her. This was a huge area of struggle for me because I wanted Bethany to meet my kids and I knew she was struggling because she hadn't yet met them. I had no idea how to make it happen. So rather than try to "make" a meeting happen, I did the only thing I knew how to do. I let go of trying to fix it and just prayed.

By some miracle, Vince's ex-wife did allow me to meet his oldest son and we picked him up and took him to a bookstore. He is high functioning autistic and sweet as can be. We gathered him up from a bowling alley and I met Vince's ex-wife at the same time. She was guarded and cold. I understood her perspective. It was evident to both of us that this blended family thing was going to be an extreme challenge. We agreed to share all our emotions, struggles, and feelings and wade in until we were ready to swim or drown, whichever the case may be. This was going to be a challenging obstacle course.

I hired a photographer to take pictures of Vince for his book cover. He was actively writing his life-changing book on losing it all and walking through the shame and struggles to rebuild your life. Jen was a school teacher and an incredible photographer. She is also, just by chance my daughter's best friend. I'm sure my daughter got an earful after the photo shoot because she swung by my house the same day to meet Vince. The wheels were slowly churning and the more we let go, God was slowly making a way where we saw no way at all.

Rarely were all the kids together at one time as my adult children were usually not home when Vince would bring his children over.

One day, I got a call that my youngest son had broken his ankle during football practice. My heart raced. My mind jumped to the worst possible scenario. Vince and I were on a date and I practically left him behind as I ran to my car, frantic, scared, and fearful. Vince said, "I'll drive you sweety." We drove to the emergency room to meet Caleb. About two minutes before we arrived, Vince leaned over to me and said, "How did Caleb get to the ER?" I said "Oh, I probably should have mentioned this, his dad brought him. You are about to meet my ex-husband."

This was going to be awkward. I figured he knew I was dating someone but we hadn't ended our fifteen year relationship on the best terms. Caleb was in a hospital bed with his dad sitting next to him. I introduced Vince as my boyfriend. Silence. My ex-husband then said hello. There are these moments in life where you want to crawl under the closest piece of furniture and this was one of them, but somehow we survived. Caleb's ankle as it turned out was not broken, but he would have to wear a boot for several weeks. What a week! We had both survived meeting the exes.

So we celebrated with a dinner celebration. Surely that was worthy of a celebratory dinner. We had survived the next step in our relationship.

Finally, the fateful day arrived when Bethany would meet my ex-wife. More importantly, she'd get to meet one of the most important people to me, my oldest son. I use the word fateful, because ex-wives and current dating partners rarely get along. Add to that my own sense of deep shame from my failed marriage. Asking for forgiveness from others was the easy part after an affair, but forgiving myself, that was another matter entirely. It took me a long while to forgive myself for all the damage I had caused to my ex-wife, my boys, and those who looked up to me. I had given myself time to heal and get healthy before dating Bethany, but there were still the lingering feelings of guilt. I had to remind myself I had already forgiven myself and my heart was changed. I was not the same man. So when I saw my ex-wife with Bethany, it was a mile marker for me. I was in a healthy relationship and was moving forward. My heart was at peace. Well, kind of.

There was still the anxiety of the first meeting with my ex-wife and my oldest son. He is such a loving soul. Having autism, he is incredibly loving and affectionate. He sees the world in a much simpler, more peaceful way. I've always envied his perspective. He gave Bethany a big hug and liked her from the start. As for my ex-wife, she was cordial towards Bethany, so that helped. The first meeting went off without a hitch, except that the other trailer, my youngest son, wasn't attached to that hitch. It would be another long six months before he would be willing to meet Bethany.

My youngest son was most aware of the affair. He had struggled with the impact of the divorce and how it had affected him. He had lost his friends and had to deal with losing the environment that he was most familiar with as we moved from Indiana back to Texas. He was adamant that he didn't want to be a part of my life with another woman in it, no matter how nice she was.

In the middle of the struggle with my youngest, I'd go on long walks. I spent a lot of time in prayer and thought. I realized that one of the most courageous things a person could ever do was forgive themselves for their failures and embrace their full worth. Living as the priceless people we are is something few ever do. Those who do it give courage to embrace that truth and live it. Having realized my value and chosen to live free from the shame and guilt of my past allowed me to be healthy mentally, emotionally, and physically. It was empowering me to love others in a healthy way. On one of my walks the thought came to me, "If I chose to embrace freedom, it could become a catalyst for my youngest son to do the same." While Bethany and I continued to date, she shared that she was struggling with not meeting my youngest son. With a deep conviction within me that my freedom would give him freedom, I reassured her it would work out.

I know sometimes she thought I was crazy thinking that, but having experienced the power of living free myself, I knew that my son would one day live free from fear and unforgiveness and choose to love and accept Bethany at the right time.

You know, one of the crazier things to me that was said to Bethany and I was "Put a ring on it!" We were told by countless people to hurry up and get married. "What are you waiting for? You've dated for six months, you know you like each other, just get married!" Can I tell you that I'm so glad we didn't. We needed to go slow and live the truth and love journey in our own way, which would also help our family work through their own issues. Due to the complexity of the blended family, we knew we needed to take time to be sensitive to each other. We would have to work through deep emotional issues all while learning how to love each other in the midst of that. One of the painful observations Bethany and I had while dating were watching the many folks who got married and divorced before we even had a chance to get engaged. We believed that taking the extra time needed on the front end of the relationship would help to create fertile soil for a solid relationship in the future.

Then came the next issue—meeting Bethany's ex-husband. In a way, Bethany was rather brilliant, or it was just coincidence, I still am not certain. I felt like I was given a two-minute notice with no time to think, "Oh yeah, you're about to meet my ex-husband." "Nice" I sarcastically thought, "thanks for the heads up!"

It actually turned out okay. Her ex-husband was a shorter guy than me, always good for the male ego. I had also come from my job in a suit. So meeting him scruffy and frumpy looking didn't hurt either for a power play. I could tell he was sizing me up so I reached out my hand, took his and shook it. "Nice to meet you" I said. I figured if I was going to meet him, I'd take the lead. He shook my hand, seeming surprised, and walked over to his son's hospital bed, waiting for the doctor to explain the damage to his foot.

The relationship was now public. We both were professional speakers, we were pretty blunt about our truth journey, and felt that we were ready to tell the world on social media and YouTube. We were putting it all out there. Here we go!

Reflection Quote:

When you choose freedom for yourself,
you choose freedom for others.

Reflections Videos: Choose Freedom-
http://bit.ly/chooseyourfreedom

Chapter 6 Reflections—The Big Reveal

- Have you gotten stuck trying to control others' reactions around you to your situation? This could be how your friends, your parents, or even how your children see your circumstances. Peace comes when you are able to let them react however they choose to.

- Can you peacefully release control over their opinions and thoughts and move forward in life with where you believe you should be despite the opinion and reaction of others?

- Have you come to a place in life where you are at peace with your past? It is difficult to move forward in the future until you are at peace with the past.

- If you have kids and you are trying to date, are you allowing them to process at their own speed and pace? True acceptance will come better if you allow them to come along on the journey at their own pace in their own way.

Chapter 7

LIVING OUT LOUD

Sitting in the sun rays on a patio at a coffee place called the Life House, we were musing over the struggles of being divorced singles. Many of our friends kept us informed of their dating struggles and it seemed that it was the norm. We had a large collection already of dating failure stories ourselves, enough to fill an entire hour of a comedy routine. We turned on our phone, pressed record and began the first video of many videos, detailing our Truth and Love Journey in dating and the dilemmas that make up the struggle for second-chance singles like us. We posted it on social media under Vince's profile. I wasn't sure I wanted it under my profile just yet. Fear still covered me as I thought about the myriad of failures that trailed behind me. This was compounded with my children's constant verbal reminders of my past failures. After this first video we joked about how embarrassing these will be if/when we break up.

We had no idea yet that these would catch on like wildfire and spread around Facebook with thousands of views, comments, letters, and requests for help. At this point of the journey we called it "The Intimacy Journey." We later renamed it the Truth and Love Journey after two seasons of videos.

The requests for help began coming in fast and furious. We began calling ourselves "the relationship non-experts." We weren't sure we should be giving advice. We had, in effect, been huge failures in our personal lives and were just starting our own journey of discovery. We decided to face dating "out in the open," transparently sharing our successes and failures with the world.

Vince is a natural counselor. His empathy for others is commendable. I on the other hand have a very corporate mindset of "suck it up and deal with it." Our combined approach became a unique combination that we were discovering freed people to pursue relationships and their purpose in a way we'd never anticipated.

It was a gorgeous day. The sun was shimmering through the trees onto Bethany's beautiful face. Her eyes captivated me. Her mind, her experiences, her passion for life were really attractive to me. I was enjoying this moment and simultaneously processing many thoughts.

I was still in the process of rebuilding my life after loosing my income, my family, and my respect as a community leader and pastor. Even though I was rebuilding my life, I still wondered if I'd ever be a leader again. I had led pretty selfishly. I began to question the motives of much of the nonprofit work that I had done. Was it for my own ego or was it for the betterment of others? These were the kinds of thoughts I shared with Bethany. She was incredibly gracious and helped me to process those thoughts in a non-judgmental way. I was on a long journey of rediscovering that my value came from simply being, not doing, a theme I was writing extensively about in my book *Child of the King*.

My emotions were still somewhat raw in this newfound freedom of learning how to just be and not perform. In the midst of that freedom, I was learning that words like authenticity, transparency, and vulnerability were powerful ways of living that could extend hope and courage for others to live free. So as Bethany and I sat outside enjoying the crisp spring air, we got into a discussion of how refreshing it was being in a relationship with someone who valued truth and vulnerability and had the courage to live both. I was thinking about how incredibly grateful I was for this woman who was different than me, yet was on the same truth journey I was on, it just came out, "Why don't we shoot a video right now? We're discovering relational secrets I never learned from two decades of counseling couples, why not share our own journey and be completely transparent about our relationship one with the other. Who knows what could happen?"

I could see Bethany's expression take on two emotions immediately. The first one was excitement. I could tell she was as adventurous as I was and loved a challenge. Then came the look of discomfort as she began to squirm a little in her chair. "So I'm not quite ready to put it on my Facebook page yet because my kids wouldn't be ready to hear everything we'd share, but if you want to post it on yours, sure, let's do it" Bethany said.

Our first video was very long, over twenty minutes, but it was very raw and real. It was the real us, sharing about how we were second-chance singles and how we were dating a new and very different way, with no attempt at charming the other. We talked about being deeply vulnerable and honest. I shared how on our first date I talked about my affair. She shared many of the relational mistakes she had made and how we were now dating in a different way. It was during the first few videos that we shot together that singles came out of nowhere, inquiring how they could experience that kind of relationship. In those first few videos we began to discover the TRUE secret to experiencing relational intimacy that's like water to a parched soul in a desert dating wasteland.

The secret is living in Truth and Love, both with ourselves and others. It's this journey that creates freedom for yourself from past fears, failures, and past emotional wounds that have been inflicted on you. Then it begins to create freedom in your relationships, leaving game playing, hiding, and creating false appearances behind. What's left is a place where there's incredible safety and security to let down your guard with the other person, and just be you. It's a place of truthful living, of sharing what you struggle with, and it creates a desire to grow. It's also a place of deep love, where all fear is removed. What's left is a place of being, of loving, of growth, of embrace, of creativity, of passion, of being fully known and still fully embraced, regardless of your faults. Part of the journey we were finding was about receiving both from our Creator and from others. Stay tuned as we share more about in the coming chapters.

Reflection Quote:

*The secret to freedom is living in Truth and Love,
both with yourself and others. This journey creates freedom
for yourself from past fears, failures, and past emotional wounds that
have been inflicted on you. Then it begins to create freedom in your
relationships, leaving game playing, hiding, and creating false appearances behind. **What's left is a place of being, of loving, of growth,
of embrace, and creativity, of passion, of being fully known and still
fully embraced, regardless of your faults.***

Reflections Videos: 1st Relational Video:
http://bit.ly/truthandlovevideo1

Chapter 7 Reflections—Showcase Videos

- Are you hiding who you really are from others?

- Do you sometimes feel that you are living a life that is as good as it will ever get? Have you accepted things as they are, believing that this is the way it has to be?

- Are you ready to be completely at peace with who you are?

- Are you ready to be vulnerable?

Chapter 8

THE TRUTH AND LOVE DISCOVERY

 The relationship that was developing with Vince was a breath of fresh air. I felt that I didn't deserve someone like him, and I kept telling him just that—over and over again. I was comfortable with abuse. It felt natural to be mistreated. Being treated with love and respect felt like wearing a pair of shoes that didn't fit. I started looking inward. Why had all my previous relationships been so hard? Why had I chosen so poorly? I began to recognize that through most of my adult life I had lived in an illusion. I saw what I wanted to see and kept quiet and ignored the obvious red flags and large blinking warning lights all around me. When dating, I would ignore red flags because I so desperately didn't want to be alone. After getting married, there were many times I would know my spouse was lying or cheating and I would simply look the other way. I am a conflict avoider and in avoiding all conflict, I created relational walls that kept out intimacy.

At dinner one night, sitting at the harbor with the sun setting in the background, Vince and I began discussing these relational perspectives. I explained that I was chasing an illusion for most of my life, a place I had been perfectly content to live in. In reality, illusion was the opposite of living in truth. Illusionary living created an "as good as it will ever get" perspective. I was either pretending all was great or I was desperately wandering around seeking something different. What developed was an ambivalence to the truth. My relationships were full of pain, hiding, and anxiety.

I thought back to a time, hiding in a bush outside of my home in California. I was as quiet as I could be. If my husband found me again, there would be a beating that could land me back in the hospital again. I held my breath, hoping he couldn't hear me. He was screaming my name while he searched for me. I was grateful the kids were not home, as the thought of them watching this horrific scene sent a chill through to my bones. They had seen us fight many times and I didn't want them to see it again. To the outside world, no one knew what was really happening behind the public façade of the perfect family we showcased every week. As I shared this with Vince, I couldn't believe what I was hearing myself say. Like clockwork, within a few hours my ex-spouse and I would both go back to pretending this didn't happen and not speak of it again. This vicious, illusionary cycle continued for years. I didn't admit to myself or others the truth that this wasn't how life was supposed to be. I shared with Vince my disgust over the abuse I had accepted. I can't believe I put my children through that. My daughter still struggles with forgiving me for the pain I put her through. That unforgiveness was an intense reminder of my shame and failure as a parent. I went on to share that, and as if that wasn't bad enough, I continued to choose these types of relationships.

As the words spilled out of my mouth, I realized how unreal it all sounded. How could someone choose poor relationships repeatedly over a lifetime? Hearing how horrid my story sounded, I threw in that I had been extremely successful in business and my work life. I used the same kind of determination that I had used for making unhealthy relationships last to drive my success at work. I conquered every difficult challenge that presented itself.

Vince thoughtfully listened and took it all in, and it was a lot to digest. I knew that Vince could see the truth of why I had made those poor decisions, I hadn't learned to value myself.

We talked about what keeps us from living in truth in relationships. Vulnerability. We avoid the truth if the information about that truth could hurt us or reveal a weakness that we are not ready to accept, admit, or try to resolve. I was ready to be vulnerable. Knowing that Vince cared about me and wouldn't purposely try to hurt me, I was ready to receive the advice and input that Vince had for me.

Because of my low self-image, these truth talks were extremely painful. In order to talk through these deep topics with Vince, I had to see my value, accept it, and listen with receptivity in order for this crazy thing to work. I felt like an explorer, venturing out to discover new lands. This was all new territory for both of us.

We drew a horizontal line from left to right, writing on the left the word illusion and we wrote the word Truth to the right on the paper in front of us:

We didn't know it at the time, but this was the beginning of the Intimacy Relational Scale that we would use in teaching intimacy and transforming relationships. For me, I just knew that I wanted to move across that line. I wanted to run from the illusion that had damaged my life and so much of my past and pursue truth with a vengeance and a passion for a new life that I was ready for. Truth would be my newfound freedom.

 I understood everything that Bethany was sharing even though I didn't have the same experiences. I had dealt with my own internal fears, anger, and self-worth issues. Looking back at my past, I realized the majority of problems I had in my early dating life started with choosing the wrong people to date because I had a poor filter or "picker" as Bethany called it. That poor picker, for me, was the result of not believing I was valuable. I had experienced decades of fear which had caused me to see relationships in a very unhealthy way. I shared with Bethany three significant issues that had affected every relationship that I'd ever had.

The first was that I believed that I was disposable. From the time I was a young child, I felt that I wasn't worth much. My parents divorced when I was six and moved to different cities. I moved in with my dad who raised me. I had occasional visits with my mother and her partner. She was experiencing a life crisis of her own and didn't know how to nurture me as a mother. This lack of nurturing left a hole that was compounded by other significant events of my childhood. Because we love others the way we love ourselves, I went through life not really knowing how to love others in a healthy way. I felt like my life didn't matter much. The result, I would come to spend decades in dating relationships and a marriage where I didn't value my partners.

The second was I was learning not to trust women. As a young child I experienced pleasure and pain through the sexual abuse done to me through a female babysitter. This caused me to objectify women to meet my needs but only if I was in control, other wise I thought they'd hurt me. The desire to be nurtured by a woman was twisted into self-gratification—looking at pornography as a young boy to meet that need. This further added fuel to the fire of objectifying women as a way of meeting my needs while never experiencing the deep need to be being completely known, accepted, and loved.

The third issue was I had also learned as a young boy that there was no one to protect me. If I didn't protect myself, then no one would. I can remember around age eight saying to myself "I will never let anyone hurt me again." So a type of prison began for me from age eight to my mid forties where my relationships would be one-sided and lonely. My friendships would be shallow because I didn't feel like I could trust people.

My dating relationships became self-centered as I would seek to get my needs met my way, manipulating situations with women for the betterment of myself. It's not that I didn't care about others. It wasn't that I didn't care about my ex-wife when I was having an affair, it's just that there was a deep hunger in my soul to be known that would never be filled because I didn't trust people enough to really open up with my thoughts and struggles. So I would go from one thing or person to try and meet that unquenchable thirst for belonging or finding value. Imagine living as a pastor and having this deep, subconscious mistrust issue. I knew I was supposed to do right thing and avoid doing wrong things. No matter how strong my will was, eventually the undealt with issues of life would pop-up.

What I believe God-fearing people sometimes don't realize is that this type of relational mistrust affects our relationship with our Creator. It becomes one-sided where it's NOT about listening and receiving, but it's only about asking to get our own needs met, most of which are quite selfish. There was a prison around me that kept me from experiencing deep vulnerability with others, and so my desire to protect myself early in childhood became a selfish, manipulative, relational wasteland that I would live in for much of my adult life.

Then, I lost everything. I recorded the story in my book *Child of the King*. Bethany had been on the journey with me while I was writing the story of loss and failure. Finally, after losing everything I was free of the fear of not trusting others because I had nothing more to hide. A new journey of freedom began for me. The removal of the resistance of not trusting others began to increase my receptivity and my ability to listen. This is why I could sit quietly while Bethany shared and receive all she had to say. I had begun a healing journey of seeing myself through God's eyes, that I was loved, valuable, and had infinite worth. I had begun to experience what it meant to be made in God's image. I had His value and worth regardless of when I was good or when I screwed up.

Being freed from fear I was beginning to love myself. As I learned how to respect and value myself, I no longer made the same poor choices about relationships, finances, and how to use my time. I was beginning to see I had a purpose and a life that mattered and my voice in those things mattered. This is what was allowing me to share all of my past failures and current struggles with Bethany.

As Bethany and I continued to write out our thoughts on that yellow piece of paper, we drew a vertical line with the word Fear at the bottom and Love at the top.

As Bethany and I shared our stories, we were learning that fear and love are the opposite of each other. I used to think love and hate were opposites. It's perfect love, as I John 4 in the Bible talks about, that removes fear. Fear is about pain, punishment, and lack. Love is about valuing, protecting, and providing. As we had only started to discover, if you value yourself, you don't allow others to mistreat you. If you value yourself, then you begin to really understand how to value other's thoughts and opinions, even if you see the situation differently. The inward journey about loving and valuing ourselves in a healthy way had pointed us towards an outward relational journey of loving, valuing, and honoring each other in a way that creates trust. Trust was becoming a fertile relational soil for the seeds of our own vulnerability. Love was removing fear. Love was creating receptivity for our growth. We were learning new ways of doing things and learning how to value each other even if we disagreed.

As we sat there watching the sun set, we were experiencing the warmness of our love for each other while feeling the warmth of the sun. It hit us all at once. Love, the life foundation that gives us the courage for truthful living, with ourselves and others, it's where the sweet spot of intimacy was that we were experiencing.

We now had, through our dinner conversation, created a relational scale that was freeing us to see the world differently. We stared at the Truth and Love Grid, plotting in our minds where we were on the scale prior to meeting and the progression that we were experiencing in our newfound relationship with each other.

We had no idea at the time that this Freedom Grid would free others to live amazing lives in their relationships the way that we were experiencing what felt like the breath of life. As we drew out the content and added adjectives, we penciled in where we used to be on the newly developed scale and where we felt we were today. We talked about what it would take to get to the relationship "intimacy sweet spot," the intersection in the upper right quadrant between Truth and Love.

We decided right then and there to not put pressure on the other person to make us happy or to meet our needs. That was a heavy burden to place on anyone. We decided to be responsible for our own attitudes, the ways we showed up in the world, and to consciously acknowledge that it was our Creator's ultimate responsibility to meet our needs, not our companions or life partners. We believed that this would free us to experience a healthy relationship.

As heavy as this moment should have been, our hearts felt light with the freedom of acceptance we felt from each other. Pounds of pressure to perform, to hide, to be someone we weren't fell away in our conversation. We were quiet for a moment as we both looked out at the sun as it set over the glistening water. There was incredible peace in my heart. I looked at this woman and saw the most beautiful, courageous, receptive person I had ever met. I was in love. I leaned in, drawing closer to her and our lips met. I felt for the first time in my life as though I was the teenager I never allowed myself to be. She leaned on my shoulder and we sat there, having had the deepest discussion, yet feeling the deepest peace. If this was what living in truth and love was all about, then this was where I wanted to live the rest of my life.

Reflections Quote:

Truth: To live in complete truth, one must have courage to live in a state of vulnerability. Have the power to be honest with yourself and others. This is the place where real intimacy has the opportunity to be experienced.

Love: This is the starting place that gives you the courage to be truthful. Love is the opposite of fear. Perfect love, as I John 4 in the Bible talks about, removes fear. Fear is about pain, punishment, and lack. Love is about valuing, protecting, and providing. If you value yourself, you don't allow others to mistreat you. If you value yourself, then you begin to really understand how to value others' thoughts and opinions, even if you see situations differently.

Chapter 8 Reflections- The Truth and Love Grid—The Relational Scale

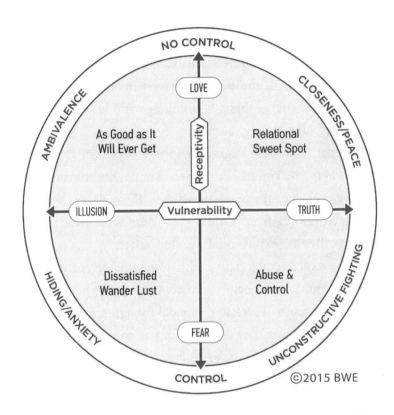

- Were there sections of Vince's or Bethany's stories that you could relate to?
    - Do you find yourself living in an illusionary or fearful life, or a combination of both?
    - If so, take time to understand where you are at and the pathways that have led you to this place.
- What will it take to move you closer to the "sweet spot"?
- You are not stuck where you are, all things can become new 2 Corinthians 5:17.

Courage for the Journey:

There is a chance that reading this chapter has released pain in your heart and brought up past wounds, leaving you feeling deflated and sad. There is power and healing on the other side of processing those feelings and understanding where they come from. These wounds, if not dealt with, erupt in our relationships like volcanos. They spew out hot lava in the form of abuse, words that harm others and cause anger. If you are experiencing these, take courage and know that this is the beginning of your healing journey.

Take heart. This is the beginning spot of your own Truth and Love journey where you can truly experience hope, healing, and freedom. From our own journey as we've worked through our issues, we've experienced healing from painful past wounds and our relationship with each other has exponentially gotten better.

If you're experiencing pain at this moment, we encourage you to seek out a counselor to help you through this journey. Wounds not dealt with can cause depression, suicidal thoughts, and sabotage relationships. This time can be different for you though. You can recover from the pains of your past. Read on as we walk through the steps towards healing and recovery and towards experiencing the best relationships you've ever had.

Chapter 9

MAKING PEACE WITH YOUR PAST

Things were going great with Bethany. We had been dating for several months and I was amazed that our relationship was going so great. I never dreamed of experiencing a relationship like the one we were having. A new fear emerged. I didn't care as much at the beginning of our relationship if it didn't work out because I wasn't as emotionally invested as I was now. If she rejected me, then it wasn't meant to be. But now the relational stakes were different. My heart was quickly attaching to this woman and I could see a life together. What if this amazing relationship I was having for some reason ended. That would be difficult. I brushed off that fear knowing the truth—didn't work out, then at least I would have experienced something amazing that I would forever carry with me.

I had some exciting things happen to me on a Tuesday morning at work, so I texted Bethany to share them. I waited 5 minutes, 10, then 30 more, but no reply. So I texted her again, thinking maybe she didn't hear my texts. No reply. I started feeling anxious and wondered if there was a reason she didn't reply. Was she mad at me? Was she talking to another guy who caught her attention? I dismissed that thought thinking how ridiculous I was being and told myself she's just busy. But several hours later at lunch she still hadn't replied, so I texted her again. After about what felt like three texts to her but really was ten, she never replied the rest of the day. I knew somehow I had screwed up. If she didn't tell me, how would I know? Why didn't she text me back?

Early that evening I gave her a call. Thank God she answered! I started with small talk to gauge her mood. She seemed fine. So I asked why she hadn't texted me. She was a bit short when I asked and said that it overwhelmed her.

At this point, the discussion could have gone several ways, many of which could have ended badly. Instead, I took the lead and assessed why was I getting anxious and I shared that with her. She shared with me why my texts overwhelmed her. It came across to her as an obsessive, controlling nature and as she'd shared previously, she was familiar with those characteristics. Talking it through, we talked about ways that we could communicate with each other that created peace for our relationship to grow.

I began to see there were deeper issues she was dealing with that were not directly about me. As I thought about that, I realized my anxiety and need to push communication with her had to do with my fear of rejection. I had been rejected a lot in my past relationships and had issues that went back to my childhood. As Bethany thought about her anxiety, she realized it came from one of her past relationships where her ex-husband would try to control her through texts, trying to make her communicate in the middle of important business meetings. We both began to see that our own soul wounds, emotional wounds we carry from past painful experiences, were triggering the soul wounds in each other. Once we saw this, we realized we needed to be aware and honest with ourselves about why we were feeling certain things. Then, we needed to share those feelings with each other. We also realized it was important to be loving, kind, and gracious with each other's struggles in those areas.

In this pivotal moment in our dating life we discovered the roller coaster ride of relationships. Both of us pointed out times in our dating pasts where things would be going well just to end up in an unexpected breakup. Many times we didn't even know the person well, but the pain that we experienced was intense. When experienced, the pain caused us to cut the person off and discontinue contact with them. Could it be that these soul wounds, when hit, are hard for us to decipher whether the pain is from the current situation or from a past relationship? We were becoming aware of how our unconscious reactions to people and situations around us resulted in the end of many dating relationships.

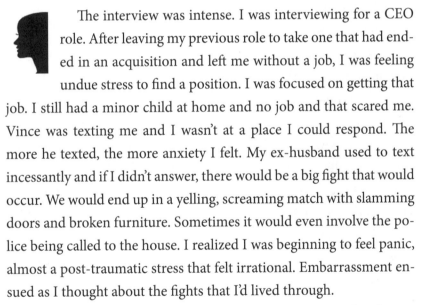 The interview was intense. I was interviewing for a CEO role. After leaving my previous role to take one that had ended in an acquisition and left me without a job, I was feeling undue stress to find a position. I was focused on getting that job. I still had a minor child at home and no job and that scared me. Vince was texting me and I wasn't at a place I could respond. The more he texted, the more anxiety I felt. My ex-husband used to text incessantly and if I didn't answer, there would be a big fight that would occur. We would end up in a yelling, screaming match with slamming doors and broken furniture. Sometimes it would even involve the police being called to the house. I realized I was beginning to feel panic, almost a post-traumatic stress that felt irrational. Embarrassment ensued as I thought about the fights that I'd lived through.

Up to this point I had been married three times. Husbands one and two were deceased, and I was divorced from husband number three. I had been beaten, physically abused to the point of hospitalization, verbally abused, had televisions thrown at me and glass vases thrown and busted. Needless to say, I was terrified of conflict. As the fear overwhelmed me, I tried to block it out. I had not known Vince long enough to have this much pain as a result of our relationship. There were simply things he did that touched my pain and brought it to the surface. Clearly I hadn't dealt with and healed from all of my past pain.

It was refreshing when we finally were able to talk on the phone. I shared my past wounds in painful detail, crying as I recanted the life that I had chosen and accepted time and time again. We decided to call these soul wounds. We prepared ourselves for the reality that even if we healed from them, there would always be these scars that if touched, would cause pain. We both recognized that we literally had to know each other so well that we could walk through life together and learn to not step on the emotional land mines that surrounded our pasts. I felt bad. I knew I had more wounds than the average human being which would mean Vince would have to be incredibly gifted at walking around the myriad of land mines that existed in my life. He explained how my reaction triggered his rejection soul wound. We began to see uniquely how dating couples scare each other away quickly, each unaware of the others pre-existing soul wounds and unknowledgeable on how to avoid them. The intense pain that is encountered when one is hit, we decided, created what we decided to call forever singles—those who think their new relationship is causing them the same pain they experienced in their painful past, avoid relationships altogether, and remain single for a lifetime.

We began to test these newfound ideas on other couples who sought us out for coaching.

One of the couples who had just started dating asked for our help. Both of them had been divorced and had children from other relationships. That's not what they were experiencing problems with, though. The primary problem for both of them was that they didn't trust each other. I took the guy out to lunch to learn more about why there was a lack of trust. He shared that he worried that she'd be unfaithful to him.

"Why do you think Nancy will be unfaithful, Bruce?"

"I don't know," he said shrugging his shoulders.

"Has she done anything that would make you think that?" I asked.

"No, it's just something I'm afraid of. Every time I share that with her, she asks me the same question. She even starts to question me, asking if there's something that I'm hiding and she gets defensive about it" Bruce shared, his eyes watering.

I can see by now the issue was not the issue. Bruce's mistrust was fueling her mistrust. The question you have to ask is "why?" Why would his mistrust cause such a strong reaction in her? I wanted to get to the real heart of the issue, and it began with Bruce.

"Bruce, what happened in your last marriage?" I asked.

He began to share about his last marriage, the struggles he had in it, and how his ex-wife had cheated on him. Ah-ha, and there it is. He doesn't trust Nancy because he believes he could re-live the pain from his last marriage. As I began to ask more questions, I also learned Nancy's ex-husband had cheated on her as well.

Both of the painful failures in their previous marriages were caused by affairs by their ex-spouses. Bruce and Nancy weren't aware that they still carried those deep relational scars. They also didn't realize it was the root of their mistrust of each other. It really had nothing to do with how either Nancy or Bruce had treated each other. It had to do with past emotional wounds causing current pain. A lack of awareness with their own issues was creating tension and mistrust in the relationship between them.

They started experiencing deep intimacy as they came to understand these issues and seek healing for their own wounds. So, rather than the breakup that was about to happen caused by their emotional past pains, they decided to work through it. They've been married for over two years now. They learned how to share the painful wounds of their pasts with each other, work through them, and be sensitive to each other's issues. They were now on the journey of experiencing an incredible relationship, even in the midst of their past baggage.

We as well were learning to be sensitive to each other's painful wounds. Our past attempts had often been to blame our mates for the pain we were feeling rather than identify if that pain had a different source. This discovery was seismic. Imagine if we could now love each other without blaming? What if we could listen intently, listening for additional puzzle pieces that make up the whole person? Could we uniquely see and hear each other, looking at the past they've lived through, the present pains and thoughts and hear their intentions not just their words? What kind of deep trust, peace, and desire to be closer to the other would be created?

For the first time in my life, I was seeing Bethany in a whole new way. It wasn't just about Bethany though. I realized my perspective was changing how I viewed and responded to others around me. I've climbed many mountains and often noticed my perspective changed the higher I got—the higher the elevation, the clearer I was able to see the path above the tree line I needed to take. This was one of many life altering perspectives that was changing me. My reactions to Bethany completely changed with this knowledge. I wanted to share everything with her, every fear, every thought, even the painful emotions I needed to process. I was beginning to experience a level of intimacy that was as good as experiencing great sex. My relationship with Bethany took a monumental leap forward and she was becoming even more desirable. I wanted to know all of her.

Reflection Quotes:

Your soul wounds, the emotional wounds you carry from past painful experiences, can cause painful experiences in your relationships. By being aware and honest with yourself as to why you feel certain things, you can begin to develop better relationships. Sharing the feelings and why you are feeling them with others will allow them to love you in a unique way.

Chapter 9 Reflections—Soul Wounds and Painful Reactions

As you were reading this chapter did you identify some of your own personal soul wounds? List them here.

_____

_____

_____

- How do you react to others around you when painful emotions of the past emerge?

- How can you explain these wounds to those close to you to help them be sensitive to your past pains?

- How can you find healing from those past wounds?

- What are ways you can be sensitive to others around you when you've accidently hit one of their soul wounds?

Chapter 10

LOVING COMMUNICATION

I realize that one of the hardest things for me is to decipher the feelings that I have and determine the root cause of those feelings. Often my anger, frustration, or intense fears that I feel towards Vince are driven by hitting a soul wound from my past. At this point in our relationship, I began to work diligently on communicating how I felt. I had experienced so much pain up to this point in my life that it had taken me years on an inward journey discovering myself to unwind some of those past pains. I had to spend time first understanding myself, then learn how to help another person learn how to know, understand, and love me.

This may sound crazy to you at first read. I would say, " I'm really hurt and angry by something you said the other night. I realize it is because you hit a soul wound. When you said what you said inferring that I had to do xyz, it hit my verbal abuse and control soul wound. Hitting this after being in abusive relationships most of my life sent me into a PTSD like depression that lasted all evening. "

That would give Vince a chance to respond. He knew right up front that loving me around these soul wounds was going to be difficult, and I knew that he wasn't responsible for the bad decisions of my past or the effects on my mental health as a result of them. In my past relationships I believed it was my mates' responsibility to intrinsically know what I was feeling without me telling them. I wanted them to know how to be sensitive to those needs. How many of you reading this know exactly what I'm talking about? You know your mate wants you to know what he/she is feeling and why.

In this brave new world of dating I decided to take the responsibility to help him understand me, to inform him of what I was feeling, and to allow him to respond and react. The unsuccessful early attempts at this in prior relationships caused me to use the silent treatment to punish him until he figured out what I was feeling or punishing him in other ways. Ironically, all of my attempts to punish him had simply left us both miserable. In one of my past relationships, every time he was mad at me or couldn't control me he would delete one of the pictures of me on his Facebook. Voilá! Fast forward a couple of years and there were no more pictures of me on his Facebook. Eventually true life mimicked the image on Facebook and I wasn't in his life anymore. These types of relational games had only created negative consequences which continued the downward spiral into failed relationships.

When I thought about avoidance, the silent treatment, withholding affection—remarkably enough, nothing helped him figure it out. Apparently mind reading is not a male trait.

So with Vince, I choose this time around to explain my feelings and chose not to hold it against him for the many days I spent in depression because of my soul wounds or if he didn't naturally understand my feelings.

A surprising thing happened. Living in this much truth and love with our communication produced peace. It removed second guessing. I didn't wonder what he was thinking or how to fix things when they went wrong. I knew he would share. I would share. We began to grow very close. I had never experienced this much peace in a relationship. As the days and months progressed, Vince learned to avoid my soul wounds. I didn't hit as many PTSD triggers. The same woman that my exes would have said was a psychotic, emotional mess was at peace, happy, easygoing and content.

I started sleeping better. Peace was filling my heart and soul. We truly began to feel like we were living in the garden of Eden. I had learned a deep truth—when I made my mates responsible for my happiness, they eventually became the enemy. When I made myself responsible for my own happiness, Vince became my intimate close friend and life partner.

Allow me to share with you the typical ingredients for what creates the average male. So imagine a man who is not sure what he's feeling other than happy, sad, or mad. Then ask him to explain why he's feeling one of those emotions. How fast can he articulate it? Is he in touch with his emotions? Good luck with getting an immediate response. Now add to that a dash of expectations that he has about life and about others close to him, caused by his life experiences and how he grew up. Then add a pound of silence. Men in America are generally trained not to express their emotions, especially if they feel raw or vulnerable. So, getting them to express their expectations based on emotions they're not entirely in touch with is very difficult. So what do you get with a man who doesn't know how to communicate what he's feeling, let alone the WHY he's feeling those emotions? You get a frustrated man who often feels like he fails at connecting in any meaningful way to the opposite sex. He's not only frustrated at his mate for not meeting his needs, he's possibly feeling frustrated at himself for not knowing why he's experiencing certain emotions and unable to articulate them. This wasn't just the average male, this was me.

After I had a long affair and it became public knowledge, I had to deal with the aftermath of devastation I caused in my previous marriage. What I dealt with wasn't just the damage to my wife, my kids, my close friends, and the loss of my job in ministry. I had to sort through what I was feeling and thinking that led to the affair and how I would heal after my own self-destructive behavior.

I remember talking to my counselor and he asked me to share what I was feeling. "I don't know, Doc?" was my reply. Then he pulled out a sheet that showed a vast amount of emotions on it. "Are you kidding me doc? There's over 400 plus emotions a person can experience?" My mouth dropped. How could I learn to identify 400 emotions when I struggled with only a few?

It took a lot of work, but as I learned how to identify what I was feeling and then learned how to share what I was feeling, I realized I shared very little in my marriage. It wasn't just that I was a slow processor with my feelings, but it was also not being able to clearly articulate those emotions with my then wife. If I felt ignored, I'd stuff that emotion because I believed she wouldn't listen to me. If I felt like she was dishonoring me, I'd tell myself I was just being emotional, and I wouldn't share how I felt.

Over time I built a huge wall of resentment towards her. Brick by brick of unspoken hurt feelings caused me to build a thick impenetrable wall of resentment towards her. My ex-wife had gone from being the love of my life to become the enemy I resented who didn't want to understand me, at least so I believed. So, ending up in an affair was only a matter of time when I found someone who did understand me. Add to that early childhood years of believing people would hurt me, and I approached all people as the enemy, where I had to manipulate them to get my needs met.

After the divorce, I tried dating, and it was terrible. It wasn't that they weren't great women, it was just that whenever they did things that hit my emotional past wounds, I quickly saw them as my enemy. I was learning through this process that it was less about them and their actions towards me and more about my failure to know what I was feeling, why I was feeling it, and share it.

When Bethany and I began dating, it was like dating for the frist time in a whole NEW way. I was sharing what I was feeling and why. I was asking her how she felt and why she was feeling it. For the first time in a relationship I understood that when I felt like Bethany hurt my feelings, she wasn't the one who created my knee jerk emotional responses. Those emotions were from my past actions and relationships and had nothing to do with her. Those were my own soul wounds and were not tied to her.

To insure that we didn't create our own soul wounds together, we were committed to sharing our feelings. Anytime we saw ourselves building a brick wall, we decided to quickly kick down the bricks through honest and loving communication. We committed to being vulnerable enough to process out loud with each other the soul wounds we were struggling with. That level of deep vulnerability could have created an immediate wound if we would have belittled or dismissed what we were sharing. But Bethany never did that. She did the opposite. She was patient with me when I had to take awhile to process what I was feeling. She was encouraging and loving when I was sharing thoughts that were dark and areas that I didn't like about myself. These intimate moments of sharing were opportunities for creating deep healing and a powerful intimate relationship that was only growing stronger. Our love and understanding of ourselves and each other created a deep security that destroyed any possibility of the other becoming the enemy.

Bethany would never be the enemy, because I had chosen to share, to understand, and to love. Our ability to communicate in this way

Chapter 10 Reflections—Loving Communication

There are four areas necessary to process through to achieve loving communication.

1. **The WHAT:** Exactly what am I feeling? Many of us are ill prepared to identify exactly what we are feeling. There are over 400 different and distinct feelings. Can you identify which of those you are experiencing? Can you pinpoint what you are feeling well enough to describe it to another? This could take a lot of introspection.

2. **The WHY:** Why are you feeling what you are feeling? If you are missing a depth of understanding of why you feel things and the real cause behind it, it causes havoc in your relationships. Any lack of internal healing or not understanding your feelings makes it difficult, if not impossible to help someone else love you because you don't even know why you are feeling what you are feeling. That expectation of he or she should understand me leaves a lot of gray between the lines of communication.

3. **The EXPECTATIONS:** What expectations do you have of your mate? What expectations have you held of your mate that may have developed over a lifetime of too many fairytale movies or too much guy talk? If you expect someone else to make you happy, you will never achieve that happiness. Lasting happiness starts from within.

4. **The ENEMY:** Have I turned my mate into the enemy? You may not realize it, but often you make your mate the enemy. You assume the worst and you blame them for failing to meet your expectations and for bad feelings that you had (not even real-izing why you have them). It is a choice to step out of a victim mindset (not believing the other person is at fault, but accepting that you own the way you react and the attitude you use when

you approach your mate) and therefore it eases the tensions and enables an easier relationship.

Chapter 11

WEAPONS OF MASS DESTRUCTION

One of the hard parts of this new relational journey was we were really retraining ourselves to do things differently and the "different" didn't seem natural or easy. What seemed natural and easy was the way we responded to situations without even thinking about them. I am a leader. I default into command and control. I want to tell others what to do and I expect them to do it. That happens during the day and I had never learned to leave the command and control me at the office. I once said to my daughter, "Conversation over." In which she replied, "I don't work for you, Mom, this is definitely not over." Now, replaying this in my mind makes me laugh out loud, but I can guarantee you that it was not at all funny to me at the time, however it does reflect the way I tried to handle conflict to no avail.

I also raise my voice when the recipient isn't responding to my liking. I get mad. I try to make things happen just like I've learned to do in my professional life. Compounded with this, I lean in towards manipulation in relationships to get my mate to do what I want them to do. This had gone on for years on end, a lifetime in effect, without my even realizing it. As I'm reading this over, part of me is thinking, "do you really want to admit all this?" I guess if we want to explain the

Truth and Love Journey to you, we have to walk down even the ugly pieces of ourselves so that you can see what the journey looks like, every aspect of it. Maybe in some ways you will see something that you can relate to or have experienced in your life.

My most common go-to is called Guilt Provoking Statements. I became very proficient at this weapon. The weapons that we pull in arguments are so natural, we often do not even see them as weapons. Not only do we not identify them as weapons but they happen as naturally as we've learned to walk and talk. So, learning to un-walk was definitely difficult. It was easy for me to say, "I went out of my way to do X, so you should go out of your way for me now to do Y" or "If you loved me you'd xyz." These weapons creep into our lives and we don't recognize them. I've seen many of my friends use the Silent Treatment to try to deal with an argument, even though that isn't one of my often-used weapons. The new me was beginning to learn to share my feelings and my hurts and pains and weaknesses and allow the other person to decide what they would do with that information. It releases all power and control and lets them either show up or not in your life, but it gives them back the power in determining how they will treat you. Whether or not they disappoint you is entirely up to them. This is a key to what love is all about letting go of controlling others and allowing them to be who they are. Love allows the other person to respond without belittling or manipulating them. In essence, as we let go of the fear that causes us to control another person, we begin to truly love them without expectations or conditions.

The old me also found it easy to use Identity Attacking Statement to change the dynamic of an argument. The brutal truth that I was now faced with was that this is a cruel and unfeeling way to treat someone. It breaks down their identity and leaves them with lowered self-esteem. It is like bludgeoning someone with a metal rod and leaving them bloody and wounded. I am sure that this sharp tongue that I used as a knife developed during the years that I was being physically abused, but nonetheless, I should have never seen this as an acceptable use of my tongue. Once identified, I had to learn to respond in a different way that left me feeling helpless and not in control. The funny truth is that I was never really in control. You cannot control another person regardless of how much you may want to. It is illusionary thinking.

Before I met Vince I had worked through many of these weapons in counseling. I was on guard against my own tongue and I was guarding it like a million-dollar bounty. I was working diligently to not let things out of my mouth in arguments until I carefully evaluated them and administered crucial judgment of the intent and the purpose behind them. Having lived for many of my years in painful reflections of the words said to me, I did not want to continue to use words to harm another person. It didn't matter what they did to me, I was in control of what I said and did in response. I still have flashbacks and very painful memories of the things said to me, cruel names I've been called and ugly statements that have marred my soul. I struggle with seeing myself as beautiful being called ugly and fat for so many years of my life. I remember seeing a movie once where the woman looked into the mirror and what she saw was different than her actual image. I struggled with having a dysmorphic view of my own image from the damage of the words said to me throughout my life. This new me, the one that was learning to see myself as beautiful because my Creator made me this way, was learning how to guard my tongue. This was the woman that Vince got to meet and I'm so thankful that he was meeting me at a time when I was learning not to react and use word weapons to attack him.

Weapons are used for deflection, control, protection or to cause harm. They are the opposite of love, vulnerability, and transparency. The key to disarming these weapons from your arsenal is recognizing that you use them, understanding why you use them, and learning how to do and say the opposite of them.

When we're emotionally healthy, we don't usually use these weapons from ill intent, but rather we use them more as defense mechanisms. We often say and do these things out of fear of not getting our needs met or fear of being hurt.

As a child growing up, I often tended to be more of a feeler than thinker. This would cause me to react to situations before reflecting on them rather than responding in an appropriate manner. Add to that, my primary love language was words of affirmation, as Gary Smalley talks about in his book *The Five Love Languages*. The people around me though didn't have that love language, and because of that could often be caustic in the words they used. When a words of affirmation person receives negative, biting, hurtful words, those words are ten times more painful than they are for another person with a different love language. Hearing hurtful words growing up as a child trained me to shut people out the moment they hit my ears. Add to that the fact that I began to deflect negative words by redirecting the focus on the other person's faults. When they said something that felt negative, I'd immediately reply with "well at least I'm not _____." If they didn't back down at this point, but reacted to my reaction, then it would eventually escalate to using the nuclear weapons option of identity attacking statements. I'd use words that would cut deep with the intention of silencing them. I can remember a lot of dating relationships I had as a teenager where I used identity attacking statements with phrases like, "you're a loser" or worse "you and your whole family are idiots. To think you could ever be in a relationship is a wonder. You have the emotional intelligence of a slug."

Do you know how world wars begin? Perspectives differ between countries, fears rise, tensions mount, threatening words escalate, and then wars begin. It's no different with relationships. I've learned first-hand, it doesn't matter how well-intentioned your heart is, the moment you use words as weapons is the moment tensions escalate and relational wars begin.

Thinking back on my first marriage, I was completely unaware of the baggage I carried into that relationship. I was so young and lacked a healthy understanding of self. My spouse carried her own issues into the marriage and was also self-unaware. I used words to deflect truthful things she said that I needed to deal with. They were painful and my knee jerk reaction was to deflect to her issues. I also had a huge control problem being an activator personality. When she didn't do things I wanted, I'd use words to manipulate her to get my own way. Not only did the deflection cause her to go silent, but resentment would grow from her as I belittled her into doing things that she didn't want to do. I was working full-time and she was a stay at home mom. I wanted the house clean. So rather than helping around the house I'd say things like "my mother does a better job at cleaning than you do." I look back at the stupid, stupid things that would come out of my young married mouth and cringe. I was so self-centered. The crazy thing was, at the time, I thought that was normal. I didn't even realize I was using words as weapons. What started as a fairytale wedding, with two people who were ready to protect each other and fight from the same foxhole, turned into two people digging their own foxholes, lobbing weaponized words at each other.

Fast forward to the present. I had come to a place of deep healing, of letting go of past hurts, of forgiving others, and even forgiving my-self for the failures I created. I had become very self-aware of what soul wounds I had and what weapons I used. While I was at a place of experiencing deep emotional healing, I also realized I had decades of negative behaviors I was going to have to unlearn. I was now conscious of my issues, now I had to be very intentional of never using relational killing weapons again.

I'd like to say Bethany met me at a time when I had learned to control my mouth and reactions, but I was still growing. Early in our dating relationship, as she went into command mode, her words often felt like judgement. When I felt that, my natural tendency was to go into self-defense mode and react with words of deflection. There was one thing I knew about Bethany though, even in the middle of feeling judgement from her. I knew she cared about me. I also knew we didn't have a history together so there really was no reason for her to judge me. Which as I thought about it meant, "Oh, perhaps she's just very straight to the point and is pointing out something that's true that I need to consider." Ding, ding, ding, ding. Give Vince Nelson a prize!

There was another dynamic at work. We both were at the point in life where truth mattered to us. We valued personal growth over our own feelings. I knew that was true about Bethany which meant we could talk through our issues together. It was safe to do so, even when we hurt the other. We went into the relationship wanting to grow personally so we would be willing to receive those words that were painful but shared with the intention of loving the other and wanting to see them grow. The other opportunity that was created by sharing and receiving truth was the opportunity to really love the other person, even when they hurt us. There is no greater opportunity for love to be experienced than when a person has been wronged and they react in a loving way as opposed to being vindictive. Bethany and I were experiencing a kind of love from each other that wasn't reactionary. We experienced this time and time again and every time we did, our intimacy would grow deeper.

Having experienced the devastating impact of using relational weapons in relationships, we want to take a deeper look at this topic.

We can't say this enough, using these weapons over time will kill your relationship. This is what broken relationships and divorces are often the result of.

When you can identify the weapons ahead of time and disarm their use, you can learn to create healthy soil for growing a magnificent relationship. You can create peace and safety that leads to rest and joy. You can create an environment that will help your mate's self-esteem because they will be able to grow and become the magnificent person they already are. By eliminating these weapons, you create a peaceful environment where intimacy can flourish.

In our beginning months of dating, we shared the deep soul wounds we both had experienced caused from our childhoods and previous relationships. We talked about what the key themes were that we would use to shut our mates down and take control.

There are many more weapons you can probably come up with, but here are the big six that we have observed people use.

• Silent Treatment

Silence becomes a deeper weapon that's a punishment that we use to control the other person. We try to punish the other person by not communicating with them. If you feel like you can't trust someone, you often just clam up and refuse to share. The Truth and Love Journey is about taking the risk. It is about being willing to walk the hard road, regardless of you wanting to be silent; it is about opening up and being willing to share. It is about creating an environment of trust so that you become a trustworthy source for sharing.

• Bringing Up Past Offenses

It is hard to listen to our faults and listen to factual examples when our faults have hurt those closest to us. That inability to receive constructive criticism often causes us to divert the attention to past offenses that were not really solved. We use these past offenses as a diversionary tactic to shift the focus away from us and avoid having to deal with the current, very painful point that is being brought up about us. Our advice is to receive. This is truly about receptivity. Try to listen. Think about the truth in the statement and reflect on what they are sharing. Be silent. Receive the words without feeling that they at any way reduce your value. You are a valuable creation and having this fault does not diminish your value.

It's important to evaluate why you feel the way you do. Why do you feel the need to divert that attention away from you? There is most probably a painful truth underneath the surface level that you must confront and understand.

• Changing Topics

We often use changing topics when we are trying to control others and we don't really want the conversation to go a certain way. You may also have a touch of Attention Deficit Disorder (ADD) and/or you haven't truly learned the art of listening.

Focus on why you are changing topics. Are you more focused on yourself than others. It may be a self-centered problem that causes one of us to NOT listen and only want to talk.

This is also a form of diversion. If you are feeling pain from the experience that is being discussed, be prepared to listen and receive. Is there validity in their statements?

• Guilt Provoking Statements

Guilt provoking statements are an attempt to control someone through manipulation by using whatever guilting type statements you can create. You try to make the other person feel that they have to do what you want them to do. You are attempting to control the end result by creating an environment that makes the other person feel like that they have to do something. When you can release this, you will feel relief. You no longer have to feel bad that they didn't do what you tried to guilt them into doing. You are learning to love them as they are, the way God made them, and allowing Him to make changes to their heart. You will not feel satisfaction in a battle to make him or make her do something.

If we can accept that God our Creator will meet our needs, we can let go of trying to make other people meet our needs.

• Passive Aggressive Words

Words and actions that are in your face and camouflage themselves as the hero of the conversation with the intent of shutting down what the other person is saying or asking for and getting your own way is a great explanation of passive aggressive words such as "because you didn't _____, I won't do _____."

They are punishing. Are you trying to punish them? What's the intent of your heart? Unresolved anger, frustration, and pain causes us to indirectly aim to hurt the other person. Our unforgiveness comes out in flippant comments that verbally sound like all is fine with in reality, both people in the conversation can tell that all is not OK.

• Identity Attacking statements

This nuclear weapon cripples your soul and the soul of the one you attack. It's a double-edged knife that cuts both ways. It's the nuclear weapon because it brings total destruction to all around, including yourself. It robs both the sender and the receiver of honor. They feel shame, and you take away negative feelings as well. This is a fast track to divorce and breakups. As the most painful and eroding of weapons, it is the equivalent of shooting the other person with a laser guided missile. They are blown to pieces and often will not recover for years to come.

You can recognize identity attacking statements because they are extremes and use the word *you* and mixed with absolute statements such as "you always, you never, you don't," or "you're always going to be a dirtbag."

If we say they are never going to change, then we are actually taking away the identity God the Creator gave them. Basically, we're stealing their Creator given identity by determining their value and how the rest of their life will go. We become God and judge. There is no grace and love in an Identity Attacking Statement. Love believes the best, not the worst, even in the face of hardship. Many of you have experienced these after a failure in your life. By not attacking their identity, you allow God to heal them and let them become a new creation. You allow God to change their heart and make them new.

When you say identity attacking statements, you are mortally wounding their souls. Most often these wounds stay with them the rest of their lives. Consider adults who are stuck in life because their parents made absolute statements about them like, "You'll never amount to anything." "You can't be a football player, you're too short." "You're not bright enough to get into college." These are the kinds of statements that, when we receive and believe what's said, limit us sometimes for the rest of our lives. We hear many in couples that we meet with says, "You will never straighten out your finances;" "You are always going to be that way" or "You will always be a failure."

These statements bring destruction to yourself. It traps you, the abuser, in shame and guilt. It causes the nuclear button pusher to forever isolate themselves from experiencing intimacy because they control all the relationships around them, which isn't love and authenticity. It's not a safe place for others to live around you, so they will naturally put up walls. They will seek others to love them unconditionally. They will feel unsafe and unloved around you. This is a hot spot for affairs and painful breakups. Everyone needs to feel honor, love, and acceptance. They need to know that someone believes in them and can see the positive even if they struggle with an issue today. To love someone, to truly love them, you have to see the value their Creator put in them despite any mistakes they have made. If you choose to use this weapon with those close to you, you'll forever live in isolation. You will live in a prison of your own creation.

Overall, when you are using any of these weapons, you're are trying to control intimacy. You're saying, if you do what I want, then I'll be close to you. But that's making intimacy conditional. Conditional intimacy isn't love. If it's conditional and not love, then it's not true intimacy. For intimacy to be real, it has to feel like a safe place to be where you won't be stabbed in the back. You can trust that your mate cares about you, even when they unintentionally use these weapons. You can work though the issue by communicating how your heart is feeling. But when intimacy becomes conditional, people shut down. Walls go up. The relationship starts to die. People seek others to meet the needs that are left barren by the destruction of the weapons.

What conditional intimacy sounds like is "don't touch me, don't get close to me." We don't normally say these things, but our body language and the quiet words we use communicate them, often VERY loudly. Imagine never pushing them away, never pulling back, but in this new world, doing the opposite of what you feel you need to do. Now we want you to pull towards them rather than away. We want you to create a safe and accepting way for them to love you and for you to love them in return.

Many of these weapons are learned in childhood and carried into adult life.

The deepest level of all of this is a belief and worldview issue. It's the belief that another person can ultimately meet your needs and that other person has the responsibility of meeting your needs. To be clear, when we believe this, we are making that other person our god. We expect that other person to be the provider of all we need. The truth is, humans will fail. With the best of intentions, we still aren't perfect and are incapable of meeting everyone's needs because (1. we can't read people's minds, (2. we have limited energy and we can't continually meet everyone's needs, (3. sometimes we're just selfish. When we can change our world view and belief and shift it to the idea that only our Creator can ultimately meet our needs, then we take that HUGE pressure off our mate. They then can simply be who they were made to be, and we will find the person again we originally fell in love with.

There are things you can do to increase intimacy and use the opposite of these weapons.

Women are manipulative by nature. Our natural tendency is if I want something is to do it for you and then hope you'll do it back. And if it's not done back, then we turn to manipulation and game playing. The way to eliminate manipulation is to simply ask for what you'd like. Use plain, clear words. And don't be offended if they choose not to. We may be surprised at how much others will do for us when we ask. Men get more of what they want because they simply ask. Women can do the same.

As a general rule, guys don't listen. Vince will vouch for this. When men don't listen, it feeds into our manipulative nature. In our minds, it is basically our guy saying to us without using words "you don't matter to me, I don't care about you." So, when I ask my guy to do something, Vince might think in his mind, "I'll do it later" but doesn't communicate when it will be done. So, I end up asking several times which makes Vince feel like I am manipulating him, but I do it because I don't feel listened to and loved. To solve this problem, if Vince would simply take out the trash when I ask, his action would communicate love and value to me. We talked about these concepts regularly while dating. They are difficult discussions because at the root of all of us is a basic human nature towards occasional stubbornness and laziness. Let's face it, we often do love our mates, but we do not really want to always do what it takes to show that love to them. That is, in truth, the most difficult part in relationships.

Another thing we noticed is that we are more likely to pick up the weapons of mass destruction when we're Hungry, Angry, Lonely or Tired. Think of the acronym H.A.L.T. Vince and I discovered and began to use this acronym for identifying when we might use a weapon before we ever do. When we're hungry, we often times feed ourselves the wrong things because we can't wait for the right things. When we're angry we react. When we're lonely, we compromise our values only to be mad at ourselves and others later for compromising. When we're tired we lose all patience and react.

The best way for both men and women to communicate their needs without using weapons is to first simply share. Share how you are feeling and ask how they are feeling. When we feel like we've been unheard or hurt, Vince and I use this simple communication tool:

"When you said/did_____, it made me feel _____. I would like you to say/do_____."

By keeping it simple and keeping the focus on how I am feeling and expressing how our mate can show us love in a way that helps us, we then slowly are working to eliminate game playing and manipulation. It requires the mate who is listening to really listen and respond in an affirmative way. This is where you can find a gold mine of experience that will create deep, lasting intimacy. By listening to how they feel, what you did that made them feel that way, and by them showing you how to love them, they've just created a pathway to their heart. This is the place where when you respond, deep connection occurs. When practiced daily, this is the place that leads to lasting depth of relationships, great sex, and a lifelong friendship.

Chapter 11 Reflections—Weapons of Mass Destruction

- Have you identified your most used weapon? List it here_____.

- Can you identify the weapon that you most dislike when it is used against you?

- Often times the pain of the weapons used on us reflect back to a place in our past where we have been deeply hurt. This is usually a great indicator that you have more healing to do in that area. If you've identified the past event that's caused you to react and use weapons in response, take some time to begin your own healing journey. Part of that may be working with a counselor or a close friend who can help you let go of the past. Part of it may be a deeper need to understand your value is not determined by anyone else's response to you. Your value is giving by your Creator and is found in His loving embrace. If you find this resonates with you, we encourage you to read Vince's book, *Child of the King*, to begin your own healing journey.

- One of the most crucial parts of this chapter is this, destroying another's identity can never be undone. Regardless of how much they have hurt you, or how much you may feel that you are only pointing out facts, attacking another's identity is the road to a quick relational death. Your relationship can possibly heal from these wounds, but it will be a very long and painful journey ahead. If you find yourself responding with weapons, then determine to eliminate these negative responses and reactions, be willing to retrain your brain and your tongue not to respond this way. Then do the deeper work of identifying why you've developed that reaction.

Kind words heal and help; cutting words wound and maim.
PROVERBS 15:4 (MSG)

Words kill, words give life; they're either poison or fruit—you choose.
PROVERBS 18:21 (MSG))

Reflections Videos: Weapons of Mass Destruction:
http://bit.ly/weaponsofdestruction

Chapter 12

THE POWER OF THE TONGUE—
FUEL OR FIRE

Bethany and I are avid hikers. We love looking for some of the most beautiful and challenging long-distance hikes we can find. From Mount Kilimanjaro in Africa, to the Annapurna Circuit in the Himalayas, to the Dolomites of Italy, to one of the most beautiful hikes in the world on the Kalalau Trail in Kauai, we love living the adventure together. One of the hikes I've always dreamed about is scaling the summit of Everest. While Bethany wouldn't do that climb, there's a little more crazy in me that has caused me to dream and study that mountain for years. This year alone eleven people have died, making it one of the most dangerous climbs in the world. So you know I'm not too crazy, I have changed my mind on climbing that mountain and am looking at less congested ones.

The interesting things about the deaths on Everest are the similar themes that emerge. Most of those who die on the mountain aren't trained and lack the endurance and mental toughness required to scale it. In fact, the most dangerous part of that climb is the decent. Some of the most common words of those who die on the mountain are "I just need to rest. I'm too tired. I can't go on." They listen to what they say and believe it. Instead of fighting to see their families back home and press on regardless of how tired or how much pain they feel, they give up. They believe their own words.

There are also similar stories of people wanting to give up but their climbing team used different words. "Get up! Dammit, you're not going to die here. Get your ass up and fight! Your family depends on you. I don't care how you feel. Get up and walk now!" Sitting in your plushy chair reading this right now you might think "those words aren't very kind." If you think that, you'd be right. But they were words of life, of love, of the greatest concern for getting their buddy down the mountain because they cared.

Words have the power of life and death. Our words have the power to take a person and cause them to give up and never move forward in life or to lift their spirits and belief in themselves to go on to create a bright and amazing future. Maybe you've had hateful, judging words spoken to you as a child like "you'll never amount to anything" or "you're no good." What we fail to see, when those words are spoken to us as children, is that we tend to believe them. We get older and we think we're worthless. So, we have to perform and prove to others we have value by being the star of that little league baseball team, or lead a lot of people, or do great things to prove that we're amazing. That was my pitfall, not believing I was worthy because of the negative words spoken to me in my childhood. Those words of judgement, of devaluing my person, caused me to live in a prison of performance for decades. I then carried that same issue into my dating life and marriage. Because I didn't believe I was worthy, I never rested. I would get annoyed with those that were laid back. I often felt like if you are not constantly busy, then you are lazy. I measured other's actions and I judged them. I thought they weren't doing enough. I thought they weren't calling enough. I thought they weren't cleaning enough. Whatever the issue was, my words to them were the same that they were to myself, "why can't you do better." Let me tell you this, it was a relationship killer.

The words of "you're not worth much" as a child cut deeply to my soul. In truth, performing to win people's approval was less of the issue. My belief that I wasn't worthy caused me to not accept myself. That was the real issue. I had to prove to myself that if I did enough, I'd be valuable. I lived in the desert wasteland of perpetual discontent where I lived without the water of peace to give rest to my soul. It wasn't until I discovered my value had nothing to do with my performance, that I could finally breath and be uniquely me.

You know, the truly interesting thing was it was the words spoken by another that lead to my freedom. With a few people close to me, they helped me see I was already valuable because I carried the value of my Creator, being made in His image. They spoke words of life to me," Vince, you matter, not because of what you could ever do. You are priceless. You are noble." Pretty soon I began to believe those words and my life changed dramatically for the positive.

Once I accepted my value, I could see the value in others. Since I believed that was I valuable without doing anything, I began to speak the same words to others that I spoke to myself. These were words of life, peace, words that affirmed a belief that you are worthy and capable.

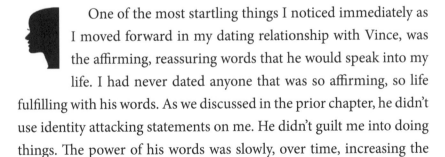 One of the most startling things I noticed immediately as I moved forward in my dating relationship with Vince, was the affirming, reassuring words that he would speak into my life. I had never dated anyone that was so affirming, so life fulfilling with his words. As we discussed in the prior chapter, he didn't use identity attacking statements on me. He didn't guilt me into doing things. The power of his words was slowly, over time, increasing the value I felt for myself.

Having lived in abusive relationships most of my adult life, I never realized the words used on me had slowly eroded my self-esteem. I felt worthless. I felt unworthy. I continued to move through life selecting dates/mates that matched my own belief system about what I felt that I was worthy of.

In my last marriage, I realized that I had developed a very sharp tongue. As I went through counseling and time with a therapist, I recognized years before I met Vince that I wanted to be different. I wanted to take the knife that was my tongue and retrain it to be life giving, and not life taking. I had let resentment build up inside of me, and that resentment would come out of me like a volcano of molten lava, burning anyone around me to a crispy critter. I had to change that if I ever wanted to have a successful and happy relationship. I had to change not only for the hope of a new relationship, but I wanted to be a different mom to my children and grandma to my grandchildren.

I slowly began to retrain my brain to speak affirmations. My love language is quality time, so speaking words of affirmation is very unnatural to me. If you haven't read the book, *The Five Love Languages* by Gary Chapman, I highly recommend it. It drove much of our thinking as we started our relationship. Both of us had read it, and we referenced it regularly. I needed to learn to carefully craft what came out of my mouth. Over time, I had begun to realize that what happens in relationships is we get angry, we punish the other person with our words, and in doing so we feel justified. I had to change my world view. I didn't need to punish others for hurting me. That was not my job nor my role. I needed to forgive. I needed to walk forward using life-affirming words towards others and seeing the good in them. I had to shift my focus from controlling them to allowing them to be whoever God made them to be. This was a hard shift for me. I had spent decades learning to be the other me.

Into this picture, Vince entered. I was beginning to shift my communication style. I was working to not use identity attacking statements. I was working on not using guilt provoking words or phrases. I had become a master of the "if you loved me, you'd do this for me" type statements. I had to release control. I had to allow them to decide what they would or would not do without my tongue lashings.

Bam! Vince stepped into my life and used affirming words and phrases and worked to uplift me. I began using affirming words to encourage him. The cyclical effect was amazing. It was like being on a constant fantasy date. I had never experienced this kind of peace. I released control. I worked to notice the sweet things Vince did for me and I'd recognize them verbally. I DID NOT mention the things I didn't like or focus on the flaws. My whole perspective shifted. We discovered that our tongues could heal the wounds inflicted by the world in the other's life if someone said something cruel at the office, we were able to talk through it and encourage each other. We became balm and healing power to each other. It became addictive. By focusing on the good things we chose to see, our minds spent more time there. Our perspectives changed. Our inner heart and souls were at peace. Neither of us imagined the power this perspective would have when it collided. It was a hundred-fold impact from what we expected. The videos we were making to talk about our relationship showcased the positive energy shining off of us. We began to impact others with our combined story.

Neither of us saw it coming. We were on individual journeys of the inward soul that then, when combined was producing a compounded effect—showcasing light to the world.

I'd like to say I came into our relationship completely healed and was perfect with every word I said, but that wouldn't be the truth. While I was aware of the performance issues and the bad behavior of measuring and judging I had carried with me for decades, I hadn't had time to unlearn that bad behavior. Early on in my relationship with Bethany I was learning her communication style. I was also learning my own. I was a words of affirmation person. Bethany was a quality time person. But Bethany was by nature a person of challenge and a strong pioneer.

Anytime she saw an opportunity for growth, she would push for it and challenge me to reach for it. I on the other hand was more of an invitational person. I liked challenge and needed challenge, but my nature was to nurture and lead through invitation. Our communication styles were often conflicting and it required a desire to understand and grow. If you're in a relationship and trying to relate to the other person in it better, you've got to be patient and willing to change the way you talk.

Until I understood our differences in those areas, Bethany's challenge oftentimes felt like judgement, even though it was always said out of love and a positive belief that I had great things ahead of me.

When I felt like I was being judged, I learned something very painful about myself. I had developed a defense mechanism where I would verbally strike out at the person who was challenging me. For example, when Bethany early in our relationship would say "you eat a lot of desserts," she was saying "I really want you to be healthy. I care about you. I had another husband die because he didn't eat right and take care of himself. I want to be with you for a life time." I heard "you're fat and over-weight."

This wasn't the problem. The problem was my unthoughtful reply of "we'll you're not looking so skinny there yourself." BOOM! The bomb had been dropped, not by Bethany but by my own stupid reaction caused by decades of poor communication skills I had learned.

Fortunately, Bethany assumed that I meant better than that and I really cared about her, which I did. So, her reaction was to say "Vince, when you said "I wasn't skinny," you were misdirecting something you thought I said and never said or meant. She would explain what she meant. To which I would give a huge apology and realize the issue in this case wasn't with her, but within me.

Over the months of dating, we would have very transparent discussions with each other when we said words that hit our previous emotional wounds. This caused us to not only understand each other, but it created a deeper closeness. As I learned more about her and how to communicate with her, I became conscious about my words. I knew she loved me, so even if I thought I heard her say something negative, I would assume she means the best for me.

My reply would be thoughtful, loving, and caring. The more interactions we had like that, where our natural reactionary words became life affirming words, believing the best about the other, an amazing thing happened.

We came out of our shells. We became more of ourselves. It was safe and peaceful being with each other. We could be crazy and be ourselves and not worry about being cut down. We were living life, and life-giving words were creating an amazing dating environment that made me want no other but Bethany. There was a time I used to notice and even gawk at beautiful women. Something strange was happening though. I stopped seeing them.

Yes, they would walk by, but the comfort, the security, and the life-giving affirmation that was being experienced, caused me to only see Bethany. She was my climbing companion who I would want on any mountain with me. If I was about to give up, she wouldn't let me. If she wanted to give up on life and her dreams, I wouldn't let her. Our words created an environment that I wanted to live in forever. Bethany was fast becoming my beautiful home.

Chapter 12 Reflections—The Power of the Tongue, Fuel or Fire

- The journey of experiencing great relationships begins with the inward soul, then it flows outward. The words we often speak to others are the words we speak to ourselves. What words do you speak to others? Do you realize you're speaking them to yourself?

- The First Challenge: For an entire week, a full seven days, we challenge you to only use positive , life affirming statements BOTH to yourself and to others. At the end of the seven days, write down how you feel. What differences did you notice in your interactions with others? Did life seem a little easier? Were others more receptive and responsive towards you in a positive way?

- The Second Challenge: How long can you do it? Can you make it a habit by doing it for an entire month? We challenge you to attempt this life changing challenge. Proverbs 4:23-24 commands us to guard our hearts. Why would God command this if it wasn't important? The challenge to speak life into your open heart will overflow positive words and life into the hearts of others.

- This is an exercise that breeds intimacy. It requires intentionality and practice.

Reflections Videos: Encouraging Your Mate:
http://bit.ly/encouragingyourmate

Chapter 13

DEEP VULNERABILITY

STOP! DON'T PUT THIS BOOK DOWN. I say that because if you're a guy like me (or even some women,) and you see the word *vulnerability* in the chapter, you might be inclined to stop reading. For men, words like transparency, vulnerability, let alone DEEP vulnerability are very uncomfortable and unfamiliar signposts in the journey of life that we're on. I used to think those words were synonymous with words like weakness, touchy feely, and effeminate.

Because of this, I tended to steer clear of them. It's not that I didn't have deep feelings and opinions about things. It's just that I had learned that to move ahead in business, I had to hide my emotions. To be able to have relationships, I had to protect myself and not reveal too much, or else women might think I'm weak and insecure. Worse than that they might reject me.

Time after time, both in high school and in college, whenever I became vulnerable with girls, I often was told I was too needy or too emotional, so I would shut down. I stopped fully sharing my emotions. I did this in my work relationships as well. Some would see this as strange because as a Christian, I believed that I should be loving, kind, thoughtful of others, and truthful. What I failed to realize was that by not being deeply vulnerable and honest with others and allowing them to see me as I was, I created an illusion of who I was.

Creating a façade of who we are is something that most people do as a result of confusion about identity, experiences, and brokenness. It's only when you understand your true identity that you can have an authentic relationship.

In my past I covered up vulnerabilities. Many men do this. We hide our true feelings from our friends.

Who they saw wasn't really me.

Who they saw instead was the person I wanted them to see. Let me tell you, after having lived that way for decades, I was exhausted and lonely. It required a lot of energy to be able to create the persona I thought others wanted me to be. It also was a slow downward spiral into greater loneliness. I felt isolated and alone, even with my best friends, girlfriends, spouse, and family. The irony is that I've seen relationships fail because one person didn't like the person the other portrayed or created. A man attracted to the girl who is over sexualizing everything, sending naked pictures, or using only sex as a lure may not want that kind of girl for a wife if he fears she'd do that with others. Most of the time attraction isn't enough to keep someone engaged forever. We were created for depth and intimacy.

As a man, let me share one of the most amazing secrets I learned after my affair, and losing my marriage and most of my friendships. Deep vulnerability isn't showing weakness, it's showing incredible strength! It takes a warrior to be truly vulnerable. It takes a person of great strength, to be secure in who they are. It also takes deep peace and a knowledge that you are priceless just as you are to find the strength to be who God made you to be.

It doesn't matter what anyone thinks. When you can get to this place, there is a tremendous power and peace in living in complete truth and love with yourself and others.

When I met Bethany and started dating her, I was at a place in my life where I was freed from decades of life sucking performance and image creation to please other people. I was done with that. I was at peace with who I was. I had an affair, I lied, I cheated, manipulated, and more, but I wasn't those things any longer. I was a person who had lost my way and did horrible things, but I was a person who was still priceless, loved, and made in the image of God. I could be honest about my past, because I had arrived at a deep place of peace with God and myself. As you're reading this book now I hope that through my story you can see how God is in the business of renovation and restoration. When you look back on your life and your decisions you'll find that your past might not resemble your current life at all. You are not that same person and you don't have to be defined by your past decisions. We all grow. That's what humans do. If you're reading this, you're on the journey to growth.

When I started dating Bethany, I was ready to just be me. It was on the phone that I shared about my affair. I shared a lot of the ugly stuff I had done. All of that happened before we ever met face-to-face. I'm not sure why I shared the truth so early but I sensed it was safe so I did.

Then when we started hanging out our truth journey continued.

I believe you've got to be whole and happy with yourself to be able to be honest with another.

I was at a place of peace with myself.

That peace empowered me to be truthful with who I was. In the traditional American dating scene, people only show their best sides (both physically and emotionally). I wondered often "would this be the day I've said too much for Bethany? Will this be the end of our relationship?" Instead, an interesting thing occurred, the more I was deeply vulnerable with her, not just with a part of my life, but with everything—my fears, my failures, my insecurities, my hopes, and my dreams—the more deeply intimacy was developing between us. I was experiencing a type of love I had never had in over four decades of my life. I was beginning to understand what the garden of Eden really was all about, being fully known and fully loved and fully embraced, while doing the same for the other.

Every fairy tale I'd ever watched had ended with "and they lived happily ever after." My life had not mimicked any fairy tale. I hadn't had the happily ever after that I felt that I had been promised each time I'd read a love story or watched a fairy tale. I had married my high school sweetheart, yes, but he had deserted me when Heather was only two years old. I had struggled as a single mom and had my heart broken again when he died. I re-married only to struggle desperately in that relationship. I was beginning to see relationships as pain. My second marriage had ended in divorce as well and I felt like I was on a losing streak not only in relationships but in life in general.

I had begun to realize that holding on to a fantasy doesn't get you closer to a great relationship. I had missed several red flags in my prior relationships. I chose to see only the good and excused away some pretty bad habits and troubles that were popping up and I don't mean kind of bad, I mean very bad. I ignored things like verbal abuse, disrespect, unloving behaviors, identity attacking statements, anger issues, addiction issues to drugs and alcohol, and issues of the heart, such as honesty, integrity, kindness, joyfulness, and spirituality.

I had fallen into a he is so wonderful syndrome. Each time I met someone, I'd see only the good, focusing on the illusions of who I wanted them to be and missing the truth of the red flags all around. Ecstasy would lead to illusion, which was a fantasy, which was basically a lie that I would buy into. I'd spent my life living lies. These lies had landed me in painful places, even once in a hospital bed with physical injuries by a person that I thought loved me. In my past relationships, we didn't really know each other. We kept the innermost thoughts from each other. We lived separate, but entangled lives.

We hid things behind curtains of our lives, keeping most thoughts secret, and not sharing everything. One such example is a man that forgot to mention in over ten years of our relationship that he had fathered a son. The illusions were grand and the information that was left out was like a giant crevasse that often felt as deep and wide as the Grand Canyon.

Now that I had experienced so much failure and loss, I had started to believe that true intimacy was born out of truth. In this newfound belief, Vince and I decided to tell all and let the chips fall where they may. This was truly the beginning of our truth journey. What we didn't expect was that sharing the hard stuff brought us closer. It was the opposite of what we expected. As we began to share from the depths of our hearts, we grew closer. Neither of us expected the other person to accept us with all our warts and faults. We learned the difference between honesty and vulnerability, and this lesson was hitting us right between the eyes.

I remember just such an example. We were sitting outside on a beautiful day. We had already shared a lot of ugliness about our pasts, our past sins, places and situations where we had made bad decisions. We shared about bad decisions that would make the other person lean towards never wanting to love us or trust us. We begin to talk about our worst sins. It is a conversation that is a very hard one to have. There are often terrible things we have done in our pasts that we don't want to admit to anyone. We feel that in keeping them to ourselves, we are safer. We don't have to risk rejection.

We decided to share our deepest part of our weaknesses and sins. It hurt. Hearing the bold truths was painful. Wondering if we could trust each other was painful. In our earthly and weak minds, we couldn't see a situation where we could love each other and continue to see the best in each other. We left that meeting feeling vulnerable and weak. We had to sleep on it.

A day later when we reconvened and discussed our feelings, remarkably we felt closer. We felt deep trust. We each felt that if the other was willing to be that vulnerable and willing to share, they were trustworthy. We grew closer despite what we thought would happen after this discovery.

Most of us think that we will find ecstasy and love by not being vulnerable. But in truth, everyone looks the same when they are pretending to be someone they are not. As you work through the fear of possible rejection, you just may find a kindred soul who will love you for who you are, not who you want to show the world you are.

We crave fantasy and illusion. We sat and watched the planet light up by *50 Shades of Gray*. The book is about a man who was sexually abused as a young man by an older woman and the scars of that abuse. He struggles to see his girlfriend as anything other than a sex object. His world view of seeing women as objects because he was treated like an object created a vicious cycle of cyclical abuse that was passed from one person to another.

People were drawn to the illusion and the physical intensity. That physical intensity is attainable when you have a deep intimate bond and throw off the beliefs that it is in any way bad to enjoy your mate's body. You may not think this is you, but many of us are passing our abused pasts onto others. Defensiveness, harsh words, protecting your own life without considering your partner's needs first. This is the human condition because humans are self-serving creatures wired for protection. But we are also loving creatures created in the image of God.

To live in that image we must each investigate our belief systems and patterns in order to be fully intimate with another. What if you saw your partner as a reflection of God in the flesh? He or she was created in His image as well.

Many of you are refusing to completely accept and love someone to the point that you deeply love them, accept them, and develop deep intimacy as God wishes for us. We decided to break that cycle and live in stark truth and love with each other.

We decided to share painful truths about our deep failures, our lapses in judgement, our sins, and our deep fears. We decided if the other person could accept all those pieces of us, then we may have our chance at our happily ever after. Once we developed that deep connection mentally and spiritually, we knew that when married we could make a deep physical connection that would be fulfilling and satisfying.

Easier said than done! As I'm writing this chapter, even having experienced this, I almost think we've made it sound too easy.

To experience deep ongoing intimacy, it takes a commitment to be deeply vulnerable daily. There's no arrival point in relationships where it's smooth sailing after you've dealt with something hard in that relationship. Relationships are a daily journey, like anything else.

Fitness isn't a one time visit to the gym and an intimate relationship isn't a one time conversation. It requires daily decisions to love, honor, and respect the other person each and every day.

You can grow deeper in your relationship, but you never fully arrive. Perhaps it could be said you arrive when you're dead, but experiencing life-long intimacy requires daily vulnerability. It starts with dealing with your own inner struggles and finding the courage to be honest with them. Then it takes the courage to share those fears, those failures, those thoughts deep inside.

Sometimes you'll be really well connected to the other person because you've shared everything up to that point, but there will always be new failures, new struggles, new fears that need to be faced and dealt with. One of the things I always tell my youngest son is to remove fears from your life, face them and walk through them.

Bethany and I were experiencing the kind of intimacy I had only dreamt about. In truth, I never realized it could be this amazing. There was one day, only maybe a month into our relationship, she shared a failure of hers that she had done that was so shameful that she had never shared it with anyone else. She was afraid I would reject her. I didn't. As she shared, I felt deep compassion for her that she had hidden that for so long. I knew what that kind of a prison was like. As she shared, I took her hand, looked her in the eyes, and said "Bethany, I love you, just as you are. What you shared doesn't change the value you hold in my eyes. You're priceless."

You would think at that moment that there would be nothing I couldn't share with her, which was true, only, I wasn't so sure it was true. I had also done things I would never speak of, way beyond the affair. They were things I felt so much shame over, I hadn't forgiven myself.

Three months later while we were on a walk, I took a moment to share my most shameful deed. She was incredibly loving and kind, but she was very, very hurt. "Months ago, I shared my most shameful moment, why didn't you? Did you think I would reject you?" I had to really think through this. "I wish I would have, Bethany, but in truth, I still struggle with forgiving myself."

Bethany embraced me, but I could tell I had hurt her. What I really did was create a false sense of intimacy. She thought I was being as vulnerable as she was. I wanted to be, but I wasn't. I was grateful she was honest with me about that. It was very painful for me to hear, but

I needed to. I was learning that to experience intimacy, you had to be courageous enough to be honest and give intimacy.

By working through my issue, Bethany actually helped me learn how to forgive myself in a deeper way. Doing the unthinkable, being deeply vulnerable, even vulnerable about my struggle with being vulnerable, created incredible intimacy with Bethany, deep peace, and freedom for my own soul to be me and be okay with that, regardless of whatever anyone else thought. Our journey of deep vulnerability together led to an inward freedom of our own souls.

Chapter 13 Reflections—Deep Vulnerability

- "Everyone looks the same when they are pretending to be someone they are not. " Are you pretending to be someone you are not? What would it take for you to be the real you?

- "To remove fears from your life, face them and walk through them."

- What fears do you have about someone close to you rejecting you based on something from your past? What pieces of your life or past have you hidden from yourself and others?

- We often have people seek us out who say, "I've never told my mate _____." If your mate agrees to go on the Truth and Love Journey with you, this is the time to share that secret from your past and to shine light in that area of your life.

Find the freedom you seek by opening up the locked doors and removing the barriers to deep vulnerability. The satisfaction and peace you will arrive at will surprise you.

Reflections Videos: Deep Vulnerability:
http://bit.ly/deepvulnerability

Chapter 14

UNIQUELY YOU

It's amusing to me that as we grow up and should be getting to know ourselves better, we somehow don't know ourselves at all. We lose ourselves. There is something about burying ourselves in work, marriages, bills, and kids that formulates a form of amnesia about who we are and our purpose and desires in life. I had raised three children, been married three times, and over the years, in my attempt to make everyone else happy I had lost myself. I was so focused on others that I didn't really know what the desires of my heart held. I thought I was unhappy with others, but if I was completely honest with myself, I would have to admit that I was unhappy with myself.

Somewhere along the road of life I had forgotten what I love to do, or simply I had become too tired in the mundane aspects of life to stop and think about who God made me to be and how I should show up in this life and be that person. At times we become chameleons who conform to the wants or needs of the people around us. It's a slow fade. You may repress your love for a certain music, or a hobby, if the one you love doesn't support or like it. You may do it unknowingly or just in the name of compromise without even being aware of your own needs until you realize you've lost a part of who you are that makes you happy. I've done this in my own life until my soul felt empty, a black-and-white version of how God created me.

Aspects of things I loved to do had been long rejected by others and so I dismissed them from my life. I had stopped being me to the fullest and only occasionally fit the things into my life I loved, which would have included painting, drawing, blogging, writing, hiking, and living the adventures that were in my heart.

God designed you to live a colorful life, not a black-and-white version.

I had become who someone else wanted me to be. I wanted to have a talk show. Many of these things seemed like crazy ideas in the hustle and bustle of my overly busy life as a working mom.

The person I had become was partying, going to bars, luxury vacationing, drinking, buying designer clothes, counting every single calorie that I intake, and being in the *in crowd*. I had been called Frankenstein when my image didn't meet standards and it had led me down a road to intense image judgement and management that was unbelievably restrictive and overpowering. There is nothing wrong with some parts of these things, there is just a realization and acceptance of who you want to be and what that life looks like for you. And then an additional realization of why you are trying to attain certain things that fall outside of who you want to be.

This reality of becoming the real me was hitting me like a steam roller. I wanted to go back to doing the things I loved. Years ago, when I had lived in California, I use to hike every weekend, taking long hikes out to amazing destinations like Kitchen Creek. I discovering trails that I would go out and hike for the weekends. I would camp out and spend time in nature, sleeping under the stars. I used to play instruments and music. It had been a big part of my early life. I had started sketching on a trip to Europe years ago and somehow, I had let that pastime slip away as well. My job, my kids, and my relationship had crept in and taken up all the crevasses of my life leaving no time and energy left for hobbies and special interests and the passions of my heart. In reality, I didn't know myself anymore. I had lost track of who I was and who I wanted to be. It had crept in so slowly over the years that I hadn't even noticed that my life was an empty shell of what it use to be. This often happens to men and women throughout their lives until they wake up one day with discontent, like the kind of urgent sadness, or despair that the author of *Wild at Heart* talks about in that poignant book for men. Reading and learning is a gift that often becomes the catalyst that can cause you to break out of your own prison or realize you're behind bars.

As I was reading the book, *Delivering Happiness*, I read about the author climbing Mount Kilimanjaro. As I read the paragraph about the author's journey to summit Kilimanjaro, my heart leapt. That sounded incredibly fun and adventuresome. I wanted to try that. Why not? I had been encouraging other people to follow their passions. I needed to take my own advice. I would sign up and do it. I started researching what it would take to climb that mountain. The thought of starting to do something that I loved again filled my heart with excitement. I had been living in a prison I'd created for myself for years. I wanted to be free, free to be who God made to be.

Vince and I hadn't known each other long when I told him I wanted to climb a mountain in Africa. I might have mentioned that it was the tallest freestanding mountain in the world. I imagined that he would think I was crazy. I had spent my life, after all, being who I thought people wanted me to be, so being myself felt very raw and vulnerable. Were women really supposed to want to climb mountains? Strange thoughts filled my mind about who I was supposed to be. Thoughts that had begun as a small child who wanted to please her parents. To my surprise Vince said, "Wow, that sounds amazing. I'd hike it with you." To my amazement, he didn't think I was crazy. At least if he did, he hid it very well. Or, maybe I had met someone that was just as crazy as I was.

Everyone else did, that's for sure.

Maybe I should stop hiding my crazy, I thought. Maybe, just maybe, someone could accept me if I chose to be uniquely me and brought that face and reality to light.

"Kilimanjaro? That's awesome. I'm in" I said to Bethany. Then I thought to myself, "she's crazy!" Here was a woman, a well put together and polished corporate executive, who knew how to where Prada well (for my guy friends reading this, that would be very expensive designer shoes). The word *crazy* did hit my mind for many reasons. I hadn't ever seen her wear hiking boots, let alone knew if she even owned any.

She had severe scoliosis as a child, a steal rod put in her back early in life, which she broke, had another put in, had her lower spine fused together and a metal cage put around it. I wondered "could she even hike a mountain?" She seemed crazy for not knowing what her physical limits were, whether she had enough stamina, and if they had Prada hiking boots. In the millisecond that it took to process what kind of crazy she was, I arrived at the thought, "She's crazy, but she's MY kind of crazy." This was a woman who loved life and was sharing things she liked to do that were a part of who I was. Would she be able to make it to the summit at 19,300 feet on the tallest free-standing mountain in the world? It didn't matter to me. What mattered is that she wanted to do the journey, and that was a journey I wanted to take with her.

Interestingly enough, while I was all in for doing that climb with her, I wasn't physically ready for it. I also wasn't emotionally ready for it. Truth was, I had lost who I was over the years. There were moments as a young boy where my spirit soared. It was camping in Boy Scouts, backpacking with my dad, rappelling off large cliffs, rock-climbing, kayaking, and rafting dangerous, class V rapids. Then there were the creative moments...doing musicals as a young boy and being recognized for my singing talents. Theater, leading contemporary worship, playing in rock bands in high school, even majoring in Opera in college were all things that I loved and excelled at. My dad had given me a gift for the love of the arts. My mom and her side of the family had blessed me with financial banking and investing skills. I was thriving in my early days.

While my soul shined in those magnificent moments of exploration and adventure as a young man, unfortunately my trust in people was diminishing. After experiencing sexual abuse as a young boy at the hands of a baby sitter, along with other adult influencers in my life who hurt me who should have been the very one's nurturing me, my heart became distrustful of others. The innocent, trusting, adventurous heart I had as a young boy and early teen turned into dark with cynicism towards the world around me. This mistrust of others created the seeds that would lead to the failure of friendships that would at best be shallow, a marriage that was hollow of real intimacy, and a coffin where my heart and dreams would die slowly over the next few decades.

With an inability to deeply connect in community, I sought value in what I could control, my performance. I excelled in singing. I was fiercely competitive, not just with card games and Monopoly, but I loved football and didn't care if teens twice my size would clobber me. If I could get one good tackle in and take them down, I was happy, no matter the amount of damage they did to me. I carried that same drive into ministry and church work. I was all about maximizing the church's mission. Let's grow it bigger! Let's create more programs. Let's grow it internationally. We can reach more people and make a bigger difference. I attempted to replace the need inside me for relationships and community with the praise of those around me acknowledging the value I created. My focus on self-validation by what I did only left my soul parched for something more. Therefore, I did more, and more, and was exhausted. My life began to crack and eventually fell apart. It's impossible to add value to the human soul by what you can do, because you were never designed as a human doing, you are a human being, made in God's image. Our value is that we are made beautiful, noble, priceless, reflecting the very image of our Creator. As a pastor for seventeen years, I totally missed that.

Fast forward after the affair, after the DWI, after the loss of friends, a good name, and family, I was left with a profound question, "Who am I?" Was I even ever a leader? What was important to me? I hadn't hiked in years. I hadn't sung in over a decade. I wasn't the dad I wanted to be. I certainly wasn't the husband I wanted to be because I was now single, created by my own failures. During that period of my life I began dating, and that turned out to be a big mistake. When you don't know who you are, others certainly won't know who you are. Many possible relationships failed to launch after the first date. Match. com, though while it worked for some people I knew, wasn't working for me. I saw attractive women, but it was just that, physically attractive pictures of women with the right measurements and basic bio, but not much more. I dated some of them but often left unsatisfied, sometimes feeling rejected because I felt no connection from them, especially when I was honest about the affair. The thought dawned on me—perhaps it's not about other people, perhaps the problem is with me.

While I was single, I slowed down on the dating scene. I began focusing on the kind of dad I wanted to be. I played Xbox with my boys, took them on little adventures, and had fun with them, teaching them through my own stories of failures. I began serving at church behind the scenes with the singles ministry, not to get noticed, but to encourage others on the journey I was on of discovering the incredible value God has given each one of us. I was in a men's group, where we were brutally honest and would share everything. In it, we also found encouragement and the courage to live in truth, acceptance, and love.

My soul, slowly, was rising up from the coffin my heart had been hidden in for decades. I was in the bathroom once and a powerful thought hit me. It sounds strange, but it felt like God Himself was saying it, "Vince, you can date any lady you want to. There's nothing wrong with that. But if you date the wrong person, a person who is not aligned to your unique purpose and where you're going in life, your life will be derailed from the incredible journey I have for you." That was incredibly deep and freeing at the same time. "Yes," I thought, "that's exactly what I want!" I wanted someone to live my purpose with. I wanted someone whose unique purpose was aligned to mine. That's when I began to discover as a second-change single that I've been given an incredible opportunity. I've been given the chance to really discover not only who I am, but what I'm passionate about and what my unique purpose is in life.

I began to live that purpose and set out to live life differently. I would be truthful with who I was, where I've been, and what I've failed at. I would be courageous and loving enough towards myself to let go of the shame of my failures and embrace that I was an influencer and leader and could use that gift in different ways to inspire others to simply be the magnificent men and women they already were.

I met Bethany, and what was an attempt to be brutally honest with who I was, no pretending, no pretense, and a miracle happened—she didn't reject me. She didn't hurt me. She was showing me love while I was being truthful. She shared in truth and how could I not embrace and love all of this beautiful, courageous woman who wanted to climb a mountain!

On this beautiful journey of intimacy, we were both experiencing, I realized another truth. In the middle of honestly, vulnerability, trust, and love—the key ingredients to the soul of cultivating relationships—birthed a new discovery of who I was and what I liked to do. Our climb up Mount Kilimanjaro was an ascent into greater freedom to be me. I discovered I was a writer, an artist, and a poet. I was learning how to use my financial skills to help people fulfil their unique purposes and dreams. As I became more uniquely who God made me to be, I became the man I wanted to be and that man was a much better mate for another.

 It takes a lot of confidence and boldness to be you and let all of you hang out without fear of reprisal or judgement. I decided I would take it as a walk of faith. As a believer in God, I never realized I questioned the foundation of human value. I grew up in church hearing "God loves you." Did I really believe that? My actions didn't show it. If they did, I would have valued myself and chosen people to be in my life who were healthy and a complement to me. It took decades to see I struggled with believing I really had value. It took even longer to arrive at the place where I finally did believe it, and my actions and who I chose to be with reflected it.

Now I was at a new place in life. If I firmly believed that my heavenly Father loved me and wanted the best for me, then He would want the best relationship for me. I had to trust that if Vince and I didn't work out because he discovered the true me, then it wasn't meant to be. I had to STOP doing what I had done my whole life, trying to make relationships happen and stop trying to control the outcome. My relationships of the past had been bitter failures. Obviously, what I was doing wasn't working. I was trying to force things to happen because I thought I wanted this guy or that guy. I didn't want to be alone and my fear of loneliness had caused me to chase relationships that were not the best for me. Now, I had no idea when I'd met them that they were not the best for me. Those realizations had come over time. As I walked through my relational past in counseling, I began to see patterns I'd repeated over and over in my life. I had missed obvious red flags. I had wanted to see the best in others, and in doing so, I had entered into relationships that I should not have. In being the best version of YOU, you drill down into who you are so deeply that you begin to understand what makes you tick. To find "the one" begins with being "the one."

It was at this stage in my life, after learning a lot about myself, when I was able to accept myself despite all my failures and mistakes. I forgave myself for each misstep. I saw the gifts God had given me and decided to love the person God had created me to be. This was incredibly freeing. I wonder how many of us have pieces of ourselves we do not like and have trouble forgiving and truly loving the person we are. It is a freeing place to be. In this place, I was confident and secure to do things I loved and fully explore the person of me. When my daughter brought up my mistakes, I was able to listen attentively and not feel like I had to defend myself. All of this to say, it put me in a position to BE THE ONE. I was able to BE THE BEST VERSION of me. I was able to be the sweet, kind, forgiving, loving, compassionate, and attentive listener that I wanted to date. Instead of looking for that healthy person, I decided I needed to be that healthy person. I switched my focus from trying to change Vince or really anyone that I would try to date, to simply being me, the person someone would want to date.

It is a change in focus. It is a redirection from outwardly focusing on what I want from others to make me whole, and how I can be the one who doesn't have to depend upon someone to make me whole. When my focus was on what I was lacking, my attitude would be glum. As I began to shift my focus to gratitude and surplus, my attitude began to reflect the gratefulness that my heart felt. I remember one day as I was moving towards this new way of thinking. I was in the grocery store. Now, having three children, and having two of them boys, a mom spends a lot of time at the grocery store. Boys eat you out of house and home. I couldn't count the number of times I've been to the grocery store. Usually I'm upset if they don't have my favorite brand, or ripe avocados. Today, I was focused on gratitude. As I walked through the stands of fruit piled high, I realized that I had enough in my checking account to pay for the groceries that I would buy. I had resources to pay for whatever I put in my basket. I didn't have to add the items up in my head as I'd done when I was a single mom all those years ago. I had forgotten through the years to even be grateful. My eyes welled up. There were rows and rows of plenty in front of me, all of which I could buy. So many years I hadn't even thought of the blessings surrounding me. I hadn't focused on these components of my life that I had taken for granted. I wanted to be the person who lived a life of gratitude. I wanted to exude joy from my being despite my circumstances. Like Paul who could celebrate being in jail, I wanted to celebrate any circumstances that surrounded me. That was the person I wanted to be. I wanted my energy to announce me into a room, not whatever else someone might notice about me. That day in the grocery store as I cried in the fruit and vegetable aisles, I realized that I wanted to be a different person than who I had been in the last few years. I wanted to live in overwhelming joy and gratefulness.

As with most things in life, it is a journey. I'd like to say that I arrived instantly at that grateful and joyous heart, but I didn't. A few months after this pivotal moment, I was invited to speak in Hawaii at a "Live your Best Life" conference. It was a mastermind event. At the end of the event in which I participated as much as spoke, the leader had us write in a notebook what it looked like to live our dreams. As I filled in the notebook page, excited about the thought of it, I felt rejuvenated. Some of the attendees read my page. One lady looked up confused.

She said, "you are already living this life." I laughed. Perspective. I was living that life. I just hadn't acknowledged it. From that day forward I decided that life was a journey and that each day I would treat it as such. I would live the fantastic life before me, recognizing that I was living my dreams. I was choosing to have the attitude and joy that made for the life I wanted. I was acknowledging the blessings before me. I was accepting that whether my life included Vince or not, I had to be the person someone would want by their side. This seismic shift in me paved the road for even more opportunities for intimacy, truth, and a journey that would land me madly in love with Vince.

I can't tell you how uncomfortable it felt. I wasn't uncomfortable with Bethany, with being honest with sharing my thoughts and feelings. I felt awkward in my own skin on this new journey of transparency with others. I was learning to live an authentic life. I had to be transparent not just with others but with myself. Much like what I was seeing happen in Bethany's life, I was seeing in mine. Did I really like all of me? No. There were still deep emotional self-inflicted wounds of shame and self-loathing that hid deep within the core of my being for the decades of selfish living I had done. In my attempt to do more and more to validate my existence to myself, I had lost who I was in the first place. Now I was on a healthy road, a journey of the inward soul to experience healing and replace decades of bad behavior I had learned. I intentionally chosen to reflect the new-found peace and belief that God says I'm loveable and priceless, and decided it was time for me to live that.

In the coffee shop, instead of grabbing my Starbucks, I intentionally made myself slow down and look around the room for the person who seemed to be open to conversation. I'd stop and say a kind word, sometimes ask a question, and it was amazing how a simple conversation would turn into a significant friendship with a guy I wouldn't normally hang out with.

I started believing that what I dreamed about could actually happen, no matter how crazy it sounded. I envisioned being a different type of leader. A leader who would impact people's lives with freedom, courage, and value. I didn't have to be a leader onstage in front of thousands, I could simply impact a life who would impact other lives. As I learned how to slow down, I began to do things that I naturally enjoyed—biking, running, working out, hiking mountains, and backpacking.

Over the many months of dating Bethany, I found I wasn't afraid to share the things I wanted to do and that were important to me. Was I afraid that she wouldn't like them or worse, think they were dumb? Yes. From sharing the greatest insecurities, I had about life and my own self-doubts, to revealing the inner nerd in me that liked science fiction, I chose to be courageous and share the real me. I did not know if Bethany would reject me or not. I was now at the point, after living in fear for decades, where I was tired and done caring if people liked me or rejected me. I thought to myself "even if she rejects me at any given point, and the relationship ends, that perhaps it wasn't meant to be." I began to see life from an abundance mindset. "If the relationship doesn't last because we don't fit well together, then perhaps it was meant to only last for a season to teach me new things." Gone was the poverty mindset of "I need to do whatever I have to do to keep her." That was a fear-based mindset and I was learning fear, scarcity, and lack go hand in hand. I was continuing to learn that powerful secret for experiencing freedom—"To erase fears from your story, walk through them." Do the opposite of what you're afraid to do. Run towards what your fear tells you to flee from.

I chose to run towards freedom. I chose to live in an abundance mindset that says "I don't have anything to fear. I am loved and priceless just the way I am." Now don't get me wrong, that doesn't mean I'm perfect. I still have decades of bad thought patterns I'm unlearning. It just means, when I screw up, I get up, ask for forgiveness of others, value myself, and keep going.

As Bethany and I were living this completely wonderful and uncharted new dating relationship together, there were and are still today so many times where our actions can hit the triggers of past wounds in the other. But rather than pulling away or fighting, we are learning to face the fear of rejection and do the opposite that we naturally feel we should do. We reach out, and we show love. We wait and don't run. Rather than revert to silence and hiding, we share when we are afraid. Living this way, no matter how hard the relationship is, cultivates deeper and deeper intimacy. It's been amazing for us.

As I live everyday with the thought of being "the one," I can tell you with all certainty, that being the one will truly help you find the one you are seeking.

Chapter 14 Reflections—Being Uniquely You

- This can be hard. Are you ready to take the journey to being uniquely you?

- List five things you love to do that you have dropped from your life in life's busyness and as the years have passed.

- To find "the one" begins with being "the one."

- How many of us have pieces of ourselves we do not like and have trouble forgiving and truly loving the person you are? It is a freeing place to be. In this place, you can be confident and secure to do things you love and fully explore the person of you.

- Overall, we suggest a change in focus to an inward focus. It is a redirection from outwardly focusing on what you want from others to make you whole, and instead you become the one who doesn't have to depend upon someone to make you whole. When your focus moves from what you are lacking, your attitude will be sad. As you began to shift your focus to gratitude and surplus, your attitude will begin to reflect the gratefulness that your heart will discover.

Reflections Videos: To Find the One, Be You:
http://bit.ly/tofindtheonebeyou

Chapter 15

THE SECRET OF THE DAILY WALK

"What do you mean it's normal?" Why is it at the point of the highs in relationships, we seem to hit speed bumps? How many of my relationships had died during the dating phase?

I had been trying to talk to Vince about his health, his eating habits, his blood pressure, his stomach problems, and his weight. He was pudgy, and the pudgy didn't bother me as much as his unhealthy eating habits did. My second husband had died of a heart attack very young, and I had a deep soul wound that encircled the importance of taking care of our bodies. I knew the difficulties of caring for a spouse that has no desire to take care of themselves and I didn't want to repeat that cycle. If I was to grow old with someone, I wanted it to be someone who wanted to care for their body and be as healthy as they could possibly be. Vince had excruciating migraines, leaving him out of it after he'd take his migraine medication. He would spend four to five times a day in the bathroom several times a day with stomach and intestinal issues. When I'd broach the subject that it wasn't normal, he would shut me down. In a calm voice one day, as we were sitting and talking about our Truth and Love Journey, I said, "Vince, I love you. I care about you. I believe that something you are doing or eating is making you sick. If we are going to fully embrace the Truth and Love

Journey, then we need to discuss this. This isn't normal." He would usually reply, "I've always been this way." Today, we had an open discussion about how we would get to the bottom of this. He listened. We talked about the importance of "the daily walk."

Just because we were able to talk about it, didn't mean he really felt the need to solve it. This debate went on for weeks. It was a cyclical argument. You have been in those—you say something, they say something, the words repeat over and over again yet never resolve. Most of us have a list of dozens of these arguments. We determined as a couple we didn't want cyclical arguments. It was a tough subject because I couldn't make a change for him, he had to want to solve this for himself. Finally, a motivation came up that got him thinking about his health. As we were talking about climbing Mount Kilimanjaro, he became interested in looking at options. He knew his joint pains and dietary problems could keep him from summitting the mountain. Imagine that even if you don't make it to the top, it is still the same expense, effort, and exhaustion. I don't think he wanted to do anything that could stand in the way of the summit. I believe that another reason he looked at options to solve this problem was because he did not want to put me through the pain of losing another man. After losing two past husbands, I was at my limit on loss. We began the long road of working to identify the issue and look at options to solve it.

It came out in our discussions one day that as a boy he had been diagnosed with an allergy to wheat. I asked him why he ate wheat every day. It wouldn't be a giant leap to say that if his body was allergic to wheat, then he probably was still today. I mentioned maybe he should try a Paleo diet. He was adamant about NOT trying a Paleo diet, but after much conversation he agreed to try a gluten free diet. Within the first six weeks of this diet, he transformed dramatically before my eyes. See Before and After Gluten Free Vince on Facebook. It was alarming in a very positive way. His body had been swelling because of the continual exposure to something his body was allergic to. His migraines reduced dramatically. His joint pain went away. He had started trying the diet because of a desire to please me, but he definitely decided to continue on the diet because of how much better his body felt without gluten. This is just one example of a struggle that we walked through on our daily journey. I know we all have them, and I believe these daily struggles are what strengthen relationships and ensure continued success, or if not solved they slowly erode our relationships and stick us in cyclical arguments. We decided to walk in complete honesty and boldly approach the struggles as they arose.

I knew from my prior relationships that falling in love hadn't been my problem. Continuing on in an exciting adventure worth living, keeping it alive and exciting had always been the problem. I now believe that a key component of this "daily walk" has to do with walking in brutal honesty and making life a daily adventure. If we were to continue our intimacy walk, we would need to share things, listen to each other in a different way, and plan extraordinary adventures even in our everyday life. We would have to walk a plan of continual courtship. We knew it would be hard. Both of us were so battle worn from distasteful and boring relationships that we were willing to go cliff jumping. This is an analogy of course since Vince is the only one of us that would really jump off a cliff.

I believe that most relationships are won or lost in the daily walk. I once read a book called *A Million Miles in a Thousand Years, How I learned to Live a Better Story*. It was about a team from Hollywood that went to do a story of a man's life. He had accomplished something movie worthy in his life and they were there to document it. They would listen to his life story and then figure out how to best document his story. What was happening in the real life story was they spent much of their time figuring out ways to better his story. If he was interested in bikes, they would say he was riding bikes in races.

Each piece of his life that he mentioned, they would add interesting components to take what he was interested in and take it up a level.

Vince and I determined that the secret of the daily walk, other than living in complete honesty included living out to the fullest the adventures God had placed in our hearts. It was about discovering what brought us joy and then expanding on that joy to bring elements of those interests into our lives. We committed to do that for each other. We would look at life as a giant Sudoku puzzle that we would grow and change and continually work to fit the numbers into the puzzle that would fulfill our hearts and allow us to live daily life adventures that were worth living. We would get outside, watch the sunsets, wake up early to bike, spend days in our pajamas, sit by a fire, and live out whatever passions were in our hearts. We embarked on an adventure that entailed an exciting daily walk full of adventures of all sorts.

I couldn't take it anymore. I stopped and threw up. I was carrying a seventy-pound backpack, I was overweight and completely out of shape. The joints in my knees were on fire, my feet hurt, and the backpack was cutting into my shoulders. What was supposed to be the one of the most beautiful and most dangerous hikes in the United States instead had turned out to be the hardest hike of my life.

The Kalalau Trail in Kauai was extraordinary. On one side of the trail was lush, green rainforest and the other side a thousand-foot drop-off walking along an extraordinary cliff. This was the place the movie Jurassic Park was filmed and we could see why. On one day we spotted five rainbows and two double rainbows. It was breathtaking, in more ways than one. I was literally out of breath the entire hike. This hike that Bethany and I were on was to prepare us for hiking Mount Kilimanjaro in Tanzania. It was eleven miles from the trailhead to the beach. You would think it was a quick hike, but it was a butt kicker. There were over sixteen accents and descents, all through four inch muddy trails where you could slip off the side of the cliff into the rocks and ocean below if you weren't careful. I was totally out of shape. This was our first real trip together, and we were learning the good and the really bad about each other. This would be a make or break trip for our relationship.

Since I was carrying all of our gear, I couldn't keep up. I was learning Bethany was "Ms. Positivity" as we would come to the crest of each accent and she would say "Great, this is easier now." I also learned that I had a tendency toward negativity as I would respond "which means that we have another grueling accent ahead of us."

She challenged me to change my perspective, even when I was throwing up. It was hard work, really hard. We finally got to our camping spot and after a quick meal, went straight to sleep. When we woke up the next morning, I was learning that it was hard for Bethany too. We were only half way in and she was exhausted and her back issues were causing significant pain.

"Vince, I'm ready to go back. I can write the trail guide for the Kalalau Trail having done this much."

"Bethany, seriously? I'm not going to allow you to write a book for the whole trail when you've only done half. Let's do this trail!"

While the daily walk was incredibly difficult on this trail, we were learning a lot about each other and ourselves. I was beginning to learn that my perspective wasn't always the right perspective. The end of the trail was worth the pain. It was like an island paradise. At the end of the trail was a beautiful beach called Lovers Beach where Bethany was able to capture one of the most spectacular photos we've ever gotten.

Fast forward a few months, we're back home and talking about climbing Mount Kilimanjaro. I was excited and scared. My body really struggled on the Kalalau Trail, and that was only eleven miles one way and no more than two thousand feet high. Mount Kilimanjaro would be seventy plus miles and nineteen thousand three hundred feet high! I had no idea how I would be able to do this. When Bethany was harping on me about my diet, it just felt like she was being negative and saying I couldn't do it because I was too fat and out of shape. That's not what she really said, but that's what I was hearing. I'd had these diet issues for decades, and I had no idea how to change it and that discouraged me.

It wasn't until she really was transparent and vulnerable with her feelings about what she experienced with her husband Nelson and the cause of his death being related to obesity, that I realized this is a real fear for her. That mattered to me. I didn't want her to be fearful as we did life together, so I was willing to try and change my diet.

As she mentioned, the transformation was extraordinary. Indeed, I was severely allergic to gluten. Not only did I lose weight and the migraines stopped, a prayer that many had prayed for decades for me to be healed from, but my gut problems went away. Six months earlier, the doctors wanted to cut a portion of my colon out because of diverticulitis. Once I dropped gluten, that problem went away. It's amazing the kind of life transformation that occurs when you're willing to listen and receive and put aside your insecurities and fears. I was learning that this wasn't a one-time deal either.

The secret to the daily walk required discipline and work. As we've said before, having healthy relationships begins with the inward journey of your own soul. It begins with looking at your perspective on life. Are you prone towards negativity when things get difficult or are you willing to focus on gratitude and stay positive? When someone who cares about you says things that are hard for your ego or fears to hear, are you courageous enough to be still, listen, and consider what they are sharing? Or, do you just detach from the relationship and shut down? The degree to which we are receptive to those around us is the degree to which we grow and change. The degree to which we receive what others are sharing is the degree to which we experience deep, fulfilling intimacy with our loved one.

The more I've learned life isn't about me, the more I've enjoyed life. The more I've let go of my need to be right in an argument, the more I grow closer to the person I care about. The more open I am to my loved one and their thoughts and feelings, the safer they feel it is to share. This is the place where intimacy thrives, even on the most difficult journeys in life.

Chapter 15 Reflections—The Secret of the Daily Walk

- Are you prone towards negativity when things get difficult or are you willing to focus on gratitude and stay positive? Your perspective combined with your receptivity is the key to transforming your daily walk.

- When someone who cares about you says things that are hard for your ego or fears to hear, are you courageous enough to be still, listen and consider what they are sharing? Or do you just detach from the relationship and shut down?

- The degree to which you are receptive to those around you is the degree to which you will grow and change. The degree to which you receive what others are sharing is the degree to which you will experience deep, fulfilling intimacy with others.

Reflections Videos: Secret of the Daily Walk:
http://bit.ly/secretofthedailywalk

Chapter 16

MAKE A LASTING LIST

I had done it. There I was in the emergency room with an arm that was extremely swollen and wouldn't move without extensive pain. Doggone it. I did not have time or room in my already too busy schedule to deal with a possible broken arm. While Vince and I were biking yesterday, I hit the brakes too hard on my new lightweight bike and I had flown over the handlebars to land on my left arm. Now I was having it x-rayed. Well, yes, it turned out it was broken. I sat watching the technician wrap my arm in the papier mâché looking wrap that I knew would harden into a cast, and I felt dismay over my situation.

As I sat there, I looked over to see Vince sitting by my bedside, there with me all the way. This was new to me. He literally walked through life alongside me despite whatever obstacle, difficulties, or the path that we had to take. I'd never had this before. I had always faced these obstacles alone. My mates hadn't wanted to be bothered or simply hadn't been able to be there for me. Their continual no-shows really said that they didn't care. I was emotionally and physically abandoned time and time again.

My mind flew swiftly back in time to the numerous hospital visits where I'd rushed to the ER late at night after a trip to have morphine shots poked into my veins due to the excruciating pain I was in with eroding disks in my back. My recollection then flies to one night where I was on IVs all night due to a bout with salmonella poisoning after a business trip. Each of those times I would sit alone in a hospital, watching the ever so white walls, with loneliness seeping into my body like a poison, slowly eating away at my heart. My mind danced around these bad memories like a game of ring-around-the-rosy. I thought of a funeral in Michigan I had attended for my cousin's son, Nick, and the extensive pain that rocked my body with him dying at the same age of my high school sweetheart, Jeff. I sat crying on the airplane on a stranger's shoulder, sobbing uncontrollably into his shirt. Each of these times, my mate wasn't there for me. I looked over at Vince. He had been there for me. He was walking through the good times and the tough times. It seemed as though he was ready to tackle whatever part of life we embarked upon. A shocking thought entered my head. Had I done this wrong my whole life? I had chosen mates and not made a "lasting list." I had prioritized the wrong things. I hadn't thought about life's journey and its ups and downs. I hadn't put loyalty, perseverance, or putting other's needs in front of their own on the top of my list of requirements for a mate. I had jumped into relationships for convenience, or had been attracted to the external appearance MORE than the internal heart and the values that they represented.

I had picked men like the Ford Agency picked models and focused solely on the external, without being worried about the qualities that made them up beneath the skin.

Vince had cared for me when I was in a car accident right after we'd met. He had been there when my youngest son Caleb's car was stuck in the mud. He was here in the ER with me. When my back pain hits a high 7 he cares for me, not complaining about what we cannot do. We use a medical scale of 1-10 when one of us in pain. It helps us to be more compassionate to the other by understanding exactly where they are. When he gets a headache, he rates the pain on a scale of 1-10 and I do the same with my back pain.

He has qualities I should have been searching for all my life, but hadn't. I hadn't made a lasting list and therefore, the men in my life hadn't been part of a lifelong journey but had been a part of fleeting moments. I always knew I loved adventurers, so I'm not sure why that wasn't a characteristic of my past mates. I highly value loyalty and honesty, and those as well were missing. Maybe I didn't value myself enough to truly demand that I locate all the things on my list before jumping into a relationship. Well not this time. At my age I now saw the pain I have caused my children and myself by not demanding that I find the right one with the right list of characteristics. I needed to run after someone that would walk through life with me, taking each part of life as an adventure.

My mom is 88, and my dad is 85. I have seen their relationship change extensively over time, simply because of the type of activities that are a part of their daily lives as they age. The older they get, the more evidence I see of the lasting list. On the phone the other day, my mom couldn't talk. Dad was about to clip her toenails and pluck her eyebrows. I laughed out loud after I hung up the phone. I was trying to imagine some of my past loves doing that for me at 88, and it was laughable. I knew they would not. It wasn't even a question. What if I had made a list for every 10 years of my life? That is what I'm recommending for you. Make a list for every 10 years. Circle anything on the list that makes it all the way to 90. Then re-prioritize your list. It should have things on the list at the top that you previously didn't see as important. What is my advice to you after all I've lived through? It would be that the list changes. In considering this, I would have done this whole dating thing entirely different.

We have more than a few single friends. Each of them is searching for their second chance after having experienced a variety of failures in their first relationships. We are watching all of these stories develop from afar. We see that many of them are trapped in the same dilemmas that we found ourselves in. They are looking for mates with their first-chance list. Their list has not changed over time. It has not morphed with life experience. They are focused on what people will think, what their Facebook profile looks like, how much money they have in the bank, what car they drive, and all the wrong things. Are you focused on their heart? Are you looking for someone with similar life passions and interests? What will it take for you to stop seeing the outside skin and start to see their inner qualities? I've often wanted to sit and interview Nick Vujacic's wife. Or sit and talk with Joni Erickson Tata's husband. Nick Vujacic is an Australian Christian evangelist and motivational speaker born with a rare disorder characterized by the absence of arms and legs. Joni Erickson Tata is a quadriplegic author, artist, singer, radio personality, and advocate for the disabled.

What do you think they saw and how did they see past the physical characteristics of Nick and Joni to fall in love with their hearts? What kind of class or life experience would allow us to truly see people for the value and individualism that makes them unique and to STOP seeing this very unimportant outer image?

As I look in the mirror daily, I am reminded over and over again that beauty is skin deep. Somehow over time we have begun focusing on the wrong things. We have been caught up in a rat race that focuses us on things that cause pain and suffering, leaving us alone and lonely. There is still someone for everyone. I believe it. I believe that there is a perfect someone for everyone. I also believe that we rule them out before we have a chance to fall in love with their hearts.

I did that. I ruled Vince out before I even met him. The only reason I journeyed on was because Tammy had introduced us. I decided to look past the stereotype of pastor and financial advisor and to truly get to know him for who is he, not who I thought he was. What would it take for you to do that? Can you make a list that sees beyond the outer characteristics and truly sees the heart?

Sitting in an Italian Riviera outdoor café, sipping on the best hot chocolate I've ever tasted, overlooking the quaint Cinque Terra town, I'm lost in thought. I'm watching the wooden speedboats gently rise and fall on the glimmering water. To my right I see mountains dotted with snow. To my left, I see the vastness of the ocean with seagulls following fiishing boats coming into port. I'm waiting on Bethany's return from her hike, a hike we both were supposed to do but due to the fever I came down with, she made the short journey on her own. I was a little worried for her, because she wasn't the best with directions, and it was starting to get late. I would continue to wait, until I knew she was safe.

My mind wandered and I thought how incredibly blessed my life was because of this woman in my life. She was an adventurer like me. She loved trying things and having new experiences. She may not be willing to jump off a cliff like I would, but she was willing to walk up to the cliff. She knew all of me. She could feel what I felt, my fears, and my thoughts. It was odd, but we both could easily read one another and there was absolutely nothing we could hide from the other. That sounded like it should be alarming and a prison, but in truth, it was the opposite. It was freedom and deep peace.

This was the first time that a person knew me completely and yet didn't recoil at the thoughts of my past failures and even moments of selfish behaviors. Don't get me wrong, she challenged me when I was acting self-centered, but she also challenged me to always be the best me that I could be. It was a place of rest and of peace. This was the woman I wanted to live out our purposes and dreams with for the rest of our lives.

I thought what kind of characteristics of the perfect woman would I want looking back from age eighty. It would be one who honors me, is a person of healthy character, is secure in who she is and her identity, who knows and is living her purpose and dreams, has a funny personality, and we click together. It would be a woman who has a deep faith and relationship with her Creator and a heart to help others. That would include pulling up my Depends™ adult diapers when I couldn't do it myself. I thought about my grandfather Walter, who for several years was taken care of by my grandmother Dorothy as his health failed. She would change his colostomy bag. I know is not the romantic thing you're thinking about when you are dating someone, but if you're going to be together for the rest of your lives, you'll later be wishing you had chosen someone who will help you through life when life is at its worst.

Did I think about those things when I was dating two girls a weekend in high school? Heck no, I was looking for the hottest girl to hang out with. Was I even thinking about those things after my separation when I began to date again? Nope. I was so wrapped up in the moment, wanting to date someone who would remove the loneliness from my life that I was compromising who I was. I was paying the price to have my immediate needs met at the expense of my purpose and future peace.

I remembered my bathroom moment and how I wanted to choose a different path, a path of living out my purpose with someone of like mindedness. This was a turning point for me where I realized I would no longer date women to fill a lonely void in my heart or to meet a momentary need, no matter how physically attractive they were. I would date as I was living my purpose, enjoying the things that I loved doing; and if the right person came into view as I was living that life, then I would be open to dating them.

From there I began thinking about the kind of list I would make. I realized that my dating/marriage list had changed over the years. When Bethany and I began dating, from the very start, we asked each other a million questions to try to get to know the other. I wanted to see how my purpose aligned with hers. The answers we found became fuel for our dreams and destiny as we found we complemented the other in powerful ways. Our brokenness from past relationships had humbled us and made us quick to listen and receive and slow to speak and command.

While a part of me wishes I would have known how to make a lasting list early in life, I was incredibly grateful that my failures and the rebuilding of my life lead me to this amazing woman who represents my lasting list.

Looking back now, I realize the secret to creating a lasting list when you're younger is to slow down, rest, receive wisdom from others, and really listen and think. What will your future self want at age 60, 70, 80, or 90? Write that down. Write down what your list is now at age 20, 30, 40. Then take the best of the later years and incorporate them into your current list. Live your dreams. Be who you really are, not who you think someone else wants you to be. If you're a second-chance single like us, then realize, "to find the one" you have to simply be you! Discover your purpose, what you're passionate are about, and what you enjoy doing. And as you do those things, you'll find the one. How do you know what "the one" looks like? To begin, don't look at the outside and what's most visible. Get to know the real person, not the person seen by the public, but the person's fears, dreams, insecurities, and character. Ask yourself, is this a person that my future 70-year-old self would want to do life with? If yes, keep sharing and learning. If not, then ask why you're dating this person and move on.

For our married friends, this can be a really tough one. Combined between the two of us, both Bethany and I have seen the worst a marriage can offer. When you're in the middle of that, how do you get to the place of living your lasting list? While there's no simple answer for this, and it may require a lot of counseling, as we've stated before, your list, like everything else, begins with your own inner soul journey. It begins with understanding what's important to you.

Then, rather than trying to get your spouse to be a certain person, why not be the person to them that's important to you? If you want to be honored, honor them, even when you may feel they don't deserve honor. If you want to be served and cherished, why not serve them and help them experience what it means to be cherished. If you need to be encouraged and affirmed, then encourage them, praising the small things they do or the unique things about them. We've found the secret to experiencing our lasting list is to live that list towards others. Leading our spouse with kindness, not coercion, goes a long way towards building closeness and intimacy. I'm grateful for Bethany, for living life with Bethany, and taking my lasting list and living that towards her.

Chapter 16 Reflections—Make a Lasting List

- Do you have a lasting list? Do you have a list at all?

- It is time to start your list today.

- Make your list for every 10 years. Start with your current decade and work upwards to 90.
    - o Circle the items that show up on every year's list.
    - o Now, make your NEW list. Moving to the top of the list the things that show up every year.
- My LASTING List

1. Fill in your NEW list here…

2.

3.

4.

5.

6.

7.

8.

9.

10.

Now as you move through life, choose to BE THE LIST for those in your life. Seek these qualities in mates that you date. Have faith and assurance and you can indeed find these qualities in another. Do not sacrifice parts of the list in fear of being lonely. Go run after your second chance!

Reflections Videos: Make A Lasting List:
http://bit.ly/createalastinglist

Chapter 17

TO FIND THE ONE, LET GO OF THE PAST

 I remember seeing a guy's jacket in Bethany's closet. "What's this? Is this one of your boy's jackets?" I asked. "No," Bethany said, "that was Jeff's jacket."

I couldn't imagine losing someone who you'd loved and was the parent of the child you had together. I assumed that was really difficult. I knew I needed to be understanding and kind because there were emotions here that I hadn't experienced. If I'm honest though, and we were on the truth and love journey, I knew I had to face my feelings and deal with them. I was a little jealous, not about a jacket. I was jealous because Bethany would sometimes go back to the past and live there for moments, longing for what she had with Jeff. I also understood that. What made it difficult is she sometimes romanticized her relationship with her first love, not being honest with the fact that he not only left her with a child, got another woman pregnant, and married this woman while he was still married to Bethany. How's that for truth and honesty.

I thought about how often I've romanticized loveless relationships because I was devaluing myself and my own dreams with thoughts of "They might have been mean towards me, but it was a good relationship. I really wanted them to know how much I loved them." How ridiculous is that thought. Notice it wasn't about how much they loved me, it was about my pursuit of them. For several past love interests in my life, they had already moved on, but sometimes I hadn't.

Having reflected on my own past behavior in the same area as what Bethany was dealing with, how could I be anything, but grace filled and understanding towards her. I shared my feelings with her. I shared that I understood and would never ask her to throw away an important part of her past. After all, it was HER past and that's what helped shape the character and nature of the woman I love today. We had agreed to live in deep truth with each other, so it wasn't just about being truthful with how I felt, it was also lovingly pointing out that the image she had of Jeff wasn't always the complete picture. As we continued to do life together, she began to acknowledge that truth.

 My high school sweetheart, Jeff Carter, was my first love. We had met when we were both young and I had fallen in love. I would crawl out my window and we would hike to the woods, exploring the natural wonder of the beauty that surrounded my house and the forest that separated his house from mine. We would talk for hours. He knew me. No one had ever known me that well. I told him all my secrets and dreams and he knew the parts of me that I hid from the world. Our relationship was, for me, the first time that I felt complete intimacy with another human being. I felt adored. I felt cherished and loved beyond belief. Four years after I met him, I moved to California with him and we married.

He made me feel totally and completely loved. I had never experienced this type of bliss. Every day seemed like a high, and our life in California was all I had ever dreamed life on the planet could be. Two years after we moved to California, we decided to have a child. Heather was such a sweet child. She really was a dream baby. Others that met her immediately began talking about having a child of their own. She was an easy baby with adorable blonde hair and a sweet personality. She was shockingly beautiful and, since I was modeling at the time, she often would do baby modeling jobs alongside me.

Jeff was overcome with all the responsibility. He wanted to live a party life, and I wasn't a partier. I was scaling heights at the medical center and moving quite quickly into a leadership role. He wanted to smoke pot, and I refused to participate, not interested in drugs, and also the knowledge of the continual drug tests I was subjected to left me less than interested in risking it all. He decided that I wasn't fun enough, that I was too serious and focused, and he left me when Heather was two years old. I held a deep pain of rejection and hurt in my heart. How could he leave me? How could he leave his adorable daughter behind? No one knew what I was facing. I didn't even tell my mother. The embarrassment was excruciating. I didn't believe in divorce, after all. I never had considered the fact that people could have been divorced who were simply pawns in the game of life, not active participants. To the world I didn't speak of any of this. I pretended all was well at home and didn't tell the executives at the hospital that I was a single parent. It was hard enough being a working female executive with a child. To the world, I skipped past this part of the story even as time passed. Jeff found another woman, moved to another state, and had a baby. We were still officially married when he returned to California and married even a different woman, a hotel maid from Los Angeles. After he married Maria, I filed for divorce.

Six years later Jeff was killed in a motorcycle accident. We had remained friends, close friends, even after his bigamy and this loss put me into a deep depression. I'm not sure I could ever completely explain this to anyone other than the one person on the planet who I felt knew me and was now dead. From this point forward, I would move directly to him dying in a motorcycle accident rather than tell the whole story. It was too painful to focus on the rejection, the betrayal, and the desertion. Heather, my daughter, called this out one day after she had reached adulthood. She said, "You say you were widowed Mom, but in reality, you were divorced." Ouch. Yes, that is true. I came to the reckoning of the absolute truth as I wrote the book *Live Your Dreams*. He had deserted me. He had found another woman. He had then found even another woman and married her while we were still married, and I had to seek a divorce. He had a baby with the woman in Minnesota, and I was left to raise our baby alone. I had thought he would always love me. I still had a tin full of love letters that I had saved from our relationship. I lived in the illusion of those brief moments when he did make me feel loved and I brushed past the total truth, too painful to face for years. I had created an exhaustive illusion.

I now realize that when we live in an illusion, we don't heal. When we hold on to the past, we stay stuck. I compared everyone to Jeff, but Vince was right. I compared them to the illusion of who I wanted to believe Jeff could have been had he not deserted me. I compared them to the moments when I had felt completely loved and safe since I had never felt that since that time. Although I married Nelson after Jeff, I continually compared him to Jeff.

Letting go of the past and focusing on the relationships in your life today prepares you for living in truth and love. I've now learned that romanticizing and fantasizing about half truths only punishes us and keeps us staring out the back window of the car that we are trying to drive forward. What we focus on expands. What we think about and concentrate on is where our focus expands. I had been focusing on a past that was gone. I cannot take it back, and I cannot re-live it. Jeff was dead. It was a bygone that could not be re-done. I became the woman I am today because Jeff was in my life, but he is now just a small piece of my past. I should have let him go years before I did. I cried over him for years. I spent time dreaming about how loved I'd felt when we were together. I had never felt that kind of love and I worked diligently to re-create it to no avail. I wanted to be unconditionally loved but I did not know how to create that type of love.

Around this time in my relationship with Vince, the movie *Fifty Shades of Grey* came out. Vince and I were surprised that the world was attracted to the illusion of the story. His girlfriend was tormented by his lack of ability to truly just love her. The world's attraction to this really showcases our attraction to illusion. We want what we want. We don't want to walk through the truth to get there. We focus on the easy path and it leads us to destruction, loneliness, and a dead-end road. I wanted out. I wanted to swim through the mote to get to a better story and I was ready to face the truth and love journey with Vince and see where this would take us.

Not focusing on the past and not comparing Vince to any of my past relationships was going to be difficult. I would need to focus on him and me. I would need to stop thinking about all the previous experiences and times, both good and bad and focus on the here and now. This was going to be the hardest journey I had taken to date.

One of the worst possible things that could happen in a relationship was happening—my ex-wife called Bethany and wanted to talk to her. Not just for a few minutes, but well over an hour. I had told my ex-wife that I wanted to introduce the kids to Bethany, and she wanted to talk to her. I knew what that meant. She wanted to tell Bethany how rotten I was and sure enough, from the other room as I overheard parts of the conversation, my ex was sharing how deeply I'd hurt her, how I would cheat on Bethany because I hadn't changed, and how I would abandon her.

At that moment I could have experienced what every other man would feel when his ex-wife calls his girlfriend—anger, resentment, frustration, and especially shame for the past affair. Oddly enough, that's not what I experienced. I was at peace with the call.

One of the deepest issues I had to come to terms with was my own past failures in my marriage and the selfishness of my heart and actions. I was really stuck there. Imagine being a pastor, knowing better and wanting to do what's right, but being so bound up with the fear, going all the way back to my childhood, that people would hurt me. I was deeply lonely. I didn't let anyone in. That deep need of wanting to be loved and known, even though I didn't trust, was the driving force behind the affair. That's the place I chose to live in illusion, letting the physical affection of another become the counterfeit replacement for real intimacy that can only be experienced through deep vulnerability.

Vulnerability was a place I was afraid to live in. So, I had an affair. After I was separated, I still wasn't willing to be vulnerable, so I dated women from online dating websites, still trying to fill the lonely void in my heart with physical intimacy, only finding that loneliness remained. As I shared in my book, *Child of the King*, it wasn't until I was completely broken and surrendered that I finally began the healing journey of being free from past fear. I was beginning to let fear of others hurting me, particularly women, go. I was now on a journey of beginning to experience authentic intimacy because for the first time I was willing to be fully known and let people all the way into my heart and soul.

That was only the first part of letting go of the past for me though. The second part was a huge mountain to climb—the mountain of shame. Once I was free of the fear, I was beginning to come to terms with the devastation I had caused not only to my ex-wife, but also the women I dated superficially, not just after my ex-wife, but even in my earlier years prior to marriage. I had a lot of shame that kept me from fully opening up and becoming transparent with another, and my ex-wife knew this, at least subconsciously.

After I began my healing journey, whenever I'd talk to my ex-wife about logistics of getting the kids, she'd invariably make comments inferring that I'd never change, that I was the same old person, still a loser and a relational failure. Her words were like prison chains that would shackle me for days to the past, keeping me stuck in depression. It took a long journey with other men in a Celebrate Recovery group, where we were completely honest about our failures that I began to see I was made in God's image. Regardless of what I did or didn't do, I am valuable because God is valuable.

As I began to embrace that newfound world view and began to let go of the world view that I was only as valuable as how I performed, I began to let go of the shame. I can even remember a conversation I had with my ex-wife at one point where she was mad at me and trying to chain me back to her past perception of me. The words that came out of my mouth surprised me, "I understand you still are mad at me, even though it was years ago that I hurt you. I'm even okay with you cussing me out because you have to work through the pain I've caused you. But if you choose to devalue me and the image God has put in me, then this conversation is done and will be done until you no longer tie me to the past." I felt deep freedom after I said that, but it wasn't just because I had cut the tie with my ex-wife. It was because I had now come to a place in life where I had received not only God's forgiveness, but I had received my own. I had let go of the past shame of my selfish actions. I was embracing the value I had and choosing to love others, even my ex-wife, when she directed anger at me.

Yes, I was hearing some of the words on the speakerphone that my ex-wife was saying to Bethany, but I was at peace. I didn't have to prove I wasn't that person anymore. I knew I wasn't. I had forgiven myself. I knew that even if Bethany rejected me, while that would hurt, it wouldn't mean I'm not valuable. On the contrary, I now chose to live in the place of valuing myself and honoring others. So, while there could still be pain if Bethany chose to live in the fear that my ex-wife still lived in, I would love her, not recoil and push her away. I would be patient.

Of course, at this point, Bethany and I both were deeply living in truth and love. There was nothing my ex-wife could say that Bethany didn't already know. There was nothing to hide and this created peace. I also knew that Bethany already knew all of me and had shown time and time again, that she still embraced me just as I was. I had never known this level of intimacy before, and my heart was at rest.

 I had come to the place where I was ready to get rid of the box of Jeff's love letters. I walked to the linen closet and dragged out the tall tin box that held the relics of my past. I had returned from dinner the previous night with a friend. Listening to her talk about calling a girl on Facebook that is dating her ex-hubsand made me think. She was trapped in the past. She wasn't with him anymore. She never would be again. She was watching his Facebook account and focusing on where he was, who he was seeing, and felt the need to rush in and rescue this woman from her ex. It wasn't up to her. The call this morning from Vince's ex-wife wasn't as alarming to me as it was to him. I knew how she felt. I was at peace with the journey we were on. I had been cheated on in the past. I knew what it felt like. I also knew that a lack of complete honesty makes for a wasteland and feeds into affairs and loneliness. I had cheated on my spouse in the past. The true journey to a great relationship begins with an inner journey, solving issues of your heart and focusing on what still hurts and why. It entails listening to yourself, wondering why you feel what you feel and exploring those feelings wherever they take you. Secrets and unshared feelings lead to devastation.

I stared at the tin box sitting in front of me on the table. It was an antique tin box from my mom. I wasn't looking forward to opening it. It sat there before me, like a pillar, and if this was a movie, I think I would have heard romantic music playing in the background. Then I would have heard a crescendo to louder music, with a drumroll. Okay, here goes. I opened the tin box and stared inside. Why is this so hard? I felt a giant lump in my throat as I peered at the pile of letters stacked about eighteen inches tall before me. I choked back the tears. I hadn't had the nerve to even open this box for over twenty-three years. I lifted a letter out of the tin. It was a letter to Jeff from me. I read a few of the words, a little embarrassed by the childlike voice of mine coming across in the letter. I picked up another, read it, and set it aside. I continued through the pile, a little alarmed that the letters are not love letters from Jeff to me, but they are letters to Jeff from me.

Was I more in love with him than he was with me? After twenty-seven letters I came to a letter to me from Jeff. I mulled it over in my hands. I read it twice. It wasn't remarkable. It wasn't something that we'd write a movie from. It didn't seep romantic lyrics or words. It was about his day and what was going on in his life. I continued through the box of letters, noticing the same unremarkable tone in all of them. Most of these letters were from me to Jeff. My box of "love letters from Jeff" as it turns out were love letters from me. I had created a mountain of illusion around how much Jeff loved me, and although I do believe he loved me, it was not at all to the extent that my fantasy story showcased. I had created the story that I wanted to remember. I had altered the facts. I had made my own fairy tale.

Illusion. Vince and I have been together for over a year now and we've already seen people get together, get married, and divorce in less than six months. Why do these things happen and why are we stuck in illusion? We've come to the conclusion that one of the main reasons is that our past unresolved soul wounds come up and are stepped on by our new relationships. People step on our past hurts, fears, insecurities, and past pains. For example, a person who was cheated on in a

Chapter 17 Reflections—Let Go of the Past

What parts of your past are you holding onto? Is there a part of your past that you are romanticizing? Are you thinking too much about a past spouse, a past boyfriend or girlfriend no longer in your life, or a spouse or relationship that has died?

What would it take for you to begin focusing on tomorrow?

Notes:

- Letting go of the past occurs on multiple levels
    - o Letting go of past hurts
    - o Letting go of your own past shame and failures
    - o Letting go of comparisons of the past
    - o Letting go of unhealthy world views and behaviors

- FOCUS: Letting go of fears and insecurities that cause unhealthy behavior: Facebook stalking, seeing who past relationships are dating, saying, doing. Learning how to forgive them, let go, and move on.

- COMPARISON: Letting go of comparing your current relationship with what you lost, rather than focusing on what you did to lose the relationship and how to grow healthier.

- INNER SHAME AND PAIN: Letting of your own relational failures and learning from them. Learning how to forgive yourself and move forward, not staying stuck there.

- TEST: When you find yourself focusing on people in your past you can't let go of or you find yourself focusing on your own failures over and over again and can't move forward, then it's time to work through those things

Reflections Videos: Let Go of the Past: http://bit.ly/letgoofyourpast

Chapter 18

LIFE PASSIONS & PURPOSE AND HOW THEY WORK TOGETHER (OR DON'T)

What do you think of when you're on the hunt to date someone? Are you thinking, "Wow, I have a great opportunity for finding someone who loves to do the things I do?" Or maybe you're thinking more altruistically "I can't wait to find someone who's passionate about the same things I'm passionate about and has the same life purpose as I do so we can make a huge difference in the world!" If you're thinking the later, then you're in the 0.01 percent of singles I've met. In my teens and twenties, I was thinking, "Look at that sexy butt!" Now you may say I'm a typical guy, but I can't tell you how many women I've met who were focused on the same thing. If it wasn't some sexy part of a person's anatomy, then they were still focused on basic needs. Let's be gut-level honest, no matter if you call yourself spiritual or a religious person of any sort, the things that we focus on are generally aligned to our basic needs—finding a person to remove the loneliness, a person to meet the physical desires that we have, or our need for deeper security and knowing our needs are taking care of. With the thousands of singles I've met, especially as a former pastor, the theme rarely changes. We're so driven by meeting our needs that we miss the bigger picture and perhaps fail to realize the unique dreams and purpose we're wired for.

Bethany and I had a friend, we'll call her Stacy, who had been single for a long time. She was physically beautiful. She was fairly emotionally healthy. More than that, she was making a huge difference helping abused women find healing and a better life. She had discovered what I call her "Popeye" moment.

If you're old enough to remember, there was a famous cartoon character named Popeye from the 1930s that came back into pop culture in the 1980s. He was a sailor who was always the underdog, fighting to win the love and affection of his sweetheart Olive Oyl, who his archnemesis Brutus was always trying to kidnap. Almost every episode Brutus would beat Popeye up and steal Olive Oyl as she yelled out "Oh help me, Popeye!" And in every episode when Popeye was at his worst, he'd utter his famous phrase "I know what I can stands, and I can't stands it no more!" That's when Popeye would open his magical can of spinach which gave him super human strength as he ate it. With forearms the size of bowling balls, he'd destroy any obstacle in his way to save Olive and win the day!

How does Popeye relate to Stacy?

Stacy was loving life. She was so thankful for where she was. She was even writing a book about her life to help others, but somewhere Stacy started focusing on the loneliness she felt. She found a guy who was relentless in wanting to date her. Who wouldn't want to date Stacy? She was amazing. The problem was, the guy, we'll call him Joe, wasn't remotely interested in the same things Stacy was. Stacy thought Joe was handsome and very charming, but it was clear where he was going in life was not where Stacy was going. He was pushing so hard to win her over, preying off her lonely feelings. There were points at which Stacy was realizing this guy was a distraction for her life. When she tried to break it off with him, he manipulated her and made her feel sorry for him with some health issues he had, playing off her desire to help others. It took Stacy years to see that she had lost herself in the relationship. She had lost sight of her purpose and the things that made her feel fulfilled. She wasn't helping women anymore. She had totally forgotten about her book. She was unhappy and had lost years in a relationship that at best was a distraction and at worst damaged her trust in men. This was a relational distraction which would take her years to recover from.

Before Joe, Stacy was living her purpose. She had found her Popeye moment! It was that defining moment when she realized her purpose and was living it. She was happy. She was on track to fulfill her destiny. But the noise of the world around her, the clamor of other people's voices and desires, coupled with the basic human needs of companionship had caused her to lose sight of her purpose.

Rather than wait and find someone who was traveling down the same road in life and aligned to her purpose, she got distracted by a momentary fix for loneliness. That need, which can be a healthy driver to help us be in community, can cripple us when not put in the greater context of who we are, what's important to us, and where we want to go in life.

While it appeared to many that I was living my Popeye moment and living my purpose, I had selected relationships that made it extremely difficult to walk that purpose path. I discovered a very important thing in my life: It is possible to choose relationships that can become constant barriers on the purpose path that God has for you. Your relationships can make it very difficult, if not impossible, to follow God's path for your life, OR you can choose a relationship where your purposes are in full alignment. In this case, the coming together of two people collides with an explosion that creates unique synergies and power beyond anything you could have envisioned before.

That is what was happening. People were messaging us on Facebook, thousands of people were watching our Facebook videos. Couples were asking to meet with us for advice and direction. We had created a tool called the Intimacy Grid that showcased the path to truth and love. Counselors began using our Intimacy Grid to help others in their counseling sessions.

Our unique combination had allowed Vince to be able to finish his book. I can't remember how many times he told me, "Thank you, I get so distracted sometimes and you really helped me focus on finishing my book."

Vince wrote a study guide titled *A 31 Day Journey of a Child of the King—Experiential Guide*. After pastoring for over seventeen years, this was his first guide book. Our time together was spent creating extensive fruit that we would have never imagined.

We started working on a Bible study titled "Discovering God and Relationships." The information was coming fast and furious from the Holy Spirit and we began to write fervently as God gave us information. We began to feel called to helping second-chance singles build incredible relationships. We started documenting the deep truths that God had revealed to us over the hours and hours that we spent together. We'd be hiking on a prep journey preparing our legs and bodies for a big climb and a deep truth would come to us as we walked. One of us would begin speaking about it and the other one would finish the thoughts. Vince was encouraging me to write and speak and be who God made me to be. This was so striking to me. I was accustomed to someone making me feel guilty about my successful endeavors, and was used to grieving each time I put a book out because of the intense difficulties caused at home. I was finally free. Not only was I living in an incredible relationship that I never felt possible, but Vince was encouraging me to live my purpose.

This played out one day when we were coming back from breakfast in downtown Dallas. We pulled into a gas station to get gas, and a lady asked me for money. I said to Vince, "God is telling me to help her." Vince replied, "See what she needs the money for." It turned out she needed to pay for her hotel charge to stay another night with her kids at a hotel. Vince said, "If you feel led to help her, I'll drive you to her hotel to pay the bill." I was so accustomed to being ridiculed and being called stupid when I felt called to help someone that his reaction surprised me. He said, "Who am I to question what you are hearing?" We drove to the hotel, and I went into the worst looking lobby I have ever seen. I wanted to cry. There were about twelve toilets sitting in the lobby, unattached. Apparently, they were upgrading the toilets and the old toilets sat in plain view alongside a bunch of other supplies in the lobby. Boy, did I feel spoiled. I was used to lobbies with marble and fountains and I felt privileged and embarrassed over the pure wealth that I am usually surrounded by. Vince was by my side and noticed the bulletproof glass on the window at the reception area. I paid for her room and we swiftly left. I sent her a text that her room was covered. As I thought over this event, I thought how fully Vince had supported me. He hadn't ridiculed me. I am not even sure that paying her hotel bill was for her, as much as it was God working on my heart. I think it could have been for me, for me to focus on another human being and to soften my heart to the needs of others. Regardless of why it happened, this one small example of how Vince supported and encouraged me became a regular occurrence as our relationship continued to develop.

The number of times that Vince accompanies me to a speaking event, driving hundreds of miles to support me, sits at a counter to sell my books, and carries boxes never ceases to amaze me. He is truly a helpmate who I could have never imagined at my side. His focus is not on making me happy. He is driven by a deep and intense desire to further the lives of others. In helping me, he is living his purpose and the combination is astounding.

You can choose someone who will enhance your purpose and passion and encourage you, igniting you in ways you never thought possible. Or you can choose a dampener, someone who consistently fights you and pulls you down, making the purpose you have in this life a never-ending battle. This sole focus, often overlooked, is the MOST VALUALBE COMPONENT on your search for a mate. Find someone who furthers your God-given purpose in life, and the fire will ignite.

I knew what my purpose was. I had spent over a decade in churches teaching how to discover your purpose. I had read and taught how to live your S.H.A.P.E. from Rick Warren's book *The Purpose Driven Life*. I believe when you fully understand who you are, you are better equipped to know how to live your life to the fullest. Learning things about the unique spiritual gifts you have—what you are passionate about, what your abilities are, what your personality type is, and how your life experiences shape you—can become the focusing lens that allows you to live with intentionality and power and create a lasting legacy.

When I met Bethany, I knew what my purpose was: helping individuals and organizations maximize their unique purposes. If you asked me my purpose, I could articulate it in a few words. But if you asked me, "How are you living your purpose based on the unique person you are?" I'd be hard pressed to give you an answer. I didn't realize how anemic and off purpose my life was. Yes, I was speaking to large groups and working for organizations that were making a difference, but I wasn't experiencing real fulfillment and excitement with living out a vision that I had. Bethany was my spinach that fueled my Popeye moment!

As we began sharing our lives together, she would ask me deep questions. "What is the vision that you see for your life and how are you living that vision, not the vision of some other person or organization?" Bethany had already developed her own exercise for discovering your purpose. She called it "The 6 Life Impact Areas." We already thought like each other.

At the time we met, I was helping lead the singles at Gateway Church in Southlake. It was scratching the surface of my desire to make a difference. What I didn't realize was, I was doing what I had always done. I was pouring all my energy into other people's visions, and helping them grow. That wasn't a bad thing, but deep within me there was a desire to lead from my own vision that God had given me. It was a vision of helping others learn their unique value, finding strength in learning how to surrender control, finding freedom to be who they really were, and living their purpose from that place.

It was effortless. Our relationship was lived from a place of honesty about what we thought and felt. There was acceptance—when life was difficult and painful, we'd be sensitive to each other. There was deep love, and Bethany loved me enough not to allow me to stay stuck in the illusion of *this is as good as life will ever get.*

I never saw that I had lived decades of my life in a scarcity mindset rooted in an identity I'd formed in my childhood, which told me I wasn't valuable. As we lived in deep truth with each other but were also sensitive to the other's fears and painful areas of vulnerability, we experienced something that just happened, life. Together we were becoming the better us, free of fear, free to dream, empowered to live out those dreams and our purposes. And the icing on the cake...we were the spinach to one another's Popeye moments!

Chapter 18 Reflections—Life's Passions and Purpose and How they work together or not

- What is your life purpose? Take time to discover it, then live it.

- If you're single, don't miss that you've been given an incredible opportunity to discover who you are, what's important to you, and what your purpose is in life. Spend time on that before you get into a serious dating relationship.

- As you're living it, date people who maximize your purpose. Ask, "What does that kind of person look like (values, life's passions, life experiences)?"

- Eliminate distractions that keep you from living your destiny.

- If you're married, being fuel for each other's purpose comes over time as you communicate what you're passionate about and share how your spouse can help you live that. It also requires you learning your spouse's purpose, asking them how you can help them live it, then encouraging them on their journey.

Chapter 19

_____

PUTTING IT ALL TOGETHER ON THE SUMMIT OF MOUNT KILIMANJARO

There is probably a good reason there are no mirrors on the mountain path we were climbing in Tanzania. It had been 5 days since I'd had a shower or put a brush through my hair, but the scenery and the adventure were exhilarating.

The climb up Mount Kilimanjaro is sixty miles that spans seven days for the route that we had chosen, the Rongai Route. It is uphill and strenuous. My physical limitations kicked in as we attempted this climb and I was struggling. As our physical bodies broke down, the hours and hours of nature and silence allowed us to process all of the life experiences that we've been through. I thought about marrying my high school sweetheart at the age of eighteen and having my daughter Heather when I was twenty. I thought of being abandoned and left to raise her alone. I re-felt the loneliness and frustration over dating in California and the inability of others to accept me as a single mom with a child. As I walked through failed relationship after failed relationship in my head, I wondered how I'd gotten to this place, to this climb, to this mountain. In a way, my whole life had been one big mountain after another. My next failed relationship left me with another child. I now was looking back across a life with three failed relationships, three children, and two of my past husbands deceased. Wow, if that isn't a mountain or two that I've climbed, I don't know what is.

Vince and I awoke at 11:00 p.m. to begin the climb at midnight to summit Mt Kilimanjaro. I was scared. This would be the hardest thing I'd ever tried to accomplish. Or would it? After surviving desertion, physical and mental abuse and divorce, and being a single mom, maybe this wasn't the hardest thing I'd ever tried to accomplish. Vince was my rock. During the six hours of continual climbing, I broke down several times. My body was aching and sore. Base camp had been above 15,000 feet, so from the beginning of our climb today our bodies had been slowly breaking down. When we finally turned around at 6:00 a.m. to see the sunrise, I felt completely spent. We watched the sun rise from the top of the world, and I felt so incredibly close to my creator. We walked across a crater and set up to tape the closing piece of our talk show episode.

When Vince knelt atop the mountain and proposed, I sat for several long moments in complete disbelief and silence. Our relationship hadn't taken extensive work. It was easier, as it turns out, to simply be ourselves. Pretending to be someone you are not takes so much work and effort. Could he really love me? Could this really be happening? As if awakened from a dream, Vince asked me again, in a much more urgent voice. "Uh, yes, yes, of course," I squeaked out. Fear filled me, could we make this work despite our records of failures? I brushed those thoughts away and headed down the mountain hand-in-hand with the man who had just proposed to me.

We were two years into dating, and we were going to be married. We hadn't rushed, and we had spent more time talking and hanging out than going on glamorous dates. We decided that once married, we would "court" each other with the fancy dinners, amazing hotels, and adventures that, for the most part, we had not done while dating.

Since we usually see the sexy side of someone while dating and then see reality after marriage, we were both looking forward to seeing the dressed-up versions of each other. We had agreed during dating to not do anything that we wouldn't do naturally (cooking, cleaning, buying flowers, etc.) and so we were not caught in any illusions about who the other person was.

The world focuses on the marriage day and the wedding. People spend months and inordinate amounts of money and resources to celebrate that one day. We chose to focus on the journey. The day of the wedding is but one day. Rather than making the wedding event the happily ever after end of the story, we wanted to make the everyday journey our happily ever after. We felt that the real work would be making that fantastical day last a lifetime. We planned a simple garden wedding at the incredible home of the amazing woman that had introduced us, Tammy Kling. We asked Pastor Inky to officiate. She was there that first night we met, so this seemed so right. My friend Jody decorated for the event and we prepared for the next mountain that we would climb—marriage. My oldest daughter and Vince's sons decided not to attend. We decided that it was okay that they journey at their own pace, but the pain we felt in their inability to be a part of this significant day weighed heavily on us.

My two boys were there with their current girlfriends. They supported me despite their fears and wonderings about whether mom was making another bad decision. I loved them for their ability to be there for me despite fears and anxieties. About fifty to seventy-five people gathered in the woods behind Tammy's house: close friends, family, and followers who had encouraged us and were there to celebrate with us. We were taking the next step in an adventure that, for all logical purposes, shouldn't have worked. We had been completely honest with each other. We had told each other painful truths about ourselves. We had revealed secrets that should have made the other person run for the hills. Why didn't we run away from each other? We decided that honesty was the most comfortable place to be. Not lying to each other made life easier. Knowing everything we thought and felt helped us to care more deeply and created an intimacy and a bond that was not easily broken. With God, the third chord of our relationship, we created the unbreakable bond that would become a lifeline to our climbing adventures together.

Onwards we marched to climbing the mountain of marriage. Who would have ever thought that this road led here? How would we ever explain the depths of the human soul and the comfort one can feel when all weaknesses are revealed? We wondered if anyone would ever believe us.

Pitch black darkness with three bouncing headlamps was all my eyes could see as I tried to find the summit of Mount Kilimanjaro above our base camp. It was 12:00 a.m. and we had begun the ascent for the summit. It was so cold, we were told to put our water bottles upside down in wool socks in the hopes that they wouldn't freeze solid in the next six hours as we made our summit attempt. As we hiked up the side of the mountain, the silence was deafening. Outside of the soft thud of hiking boots on the frozen volcanic scree we were climbing on and the sound of my own breath, it was deathly quiet. There was nothing else to do but take the next step and think. Due to the high elevation and the fatigue of the journey, no one was talking. For over six hours of arduous hiking, I reflected back on my life and looked at how far I had come. I had gained so much and lost it all because of the incredible childhood fear of being hurt by others that short-circuited my ability to experience deep intimacy. I made an inner vow after my childhood sexual abuse that I would never allow anyone to hurt me again. What I didn't realize was, I continued to protect my heart the same way into my adult life. I did the very thing C.S. Lewis said you could do to protect your heart. I hadn't allowed myself to experience vulnerability.

> *To love at all is to be vulnerable. Love anything and your heart will be wrung and possibly broken. If you want to make sure of keeping it intact you must give it to no one, not even an animal. Wrap it carefully round with hobbies and little luxuries; avoid all entanglements. Lock it up safe in the casket or coffin of your selfishness. But in that casket, safe, dark, motionless, airless, it will change. It will not be broken; it will become unbreakable, impenetrable, irredeemable. To love is to be vulnerable.*
> C.S. LEWIS, THE FOUR LOVES

That protection created shallow friendships of knowing others but never allowing others to know the real me. It created a marriage that was destined for failure caused by an inability to connect in the deepest way that the human soul was designed for. It led to the affair that killed my marriage, created by my own selfish attempt to fill the lonely void in my heart. Fearful living and decisions combined with a self-made image of a successful man collapsed like a house built with a deck of cards. Each card represented my lies to myself: I didn't need people. People couldn't be trusted. I could meet my own needs. I wasn't valuable, so I had to prove to myself that I was. The more I did, the more valuable I'd be, or so I had thought. That was an illusionary life I didn't have the strength to continue, so it all imploded. I had gone from the summit of life to the valley of destruction, where I lost everything.

There was a point at which I had given up on my dreams and on life itself. An interesting thing happened though. When I stopped hiding, my heart began to grow. I began to gain real friendships with men who knew me, accepted me, and encouraged me to grow. I began treating women not as objects, but as valuable human beings. I began to dream again, to do the things I really enjoyed. I no longer had to please other people. I no longer had to prove my worth, I was already valuable because I was loved by God and made in His priceless image. One of the most powerful truths that Bethany often shares with me is "The mountain is in your head." I had learned how to finally summit that mountain.

The journey up Mount Kilimanjaro was a letting go of the past and an embrace of my current and future journey, a journey walking hand-in-hand with this magnificent woman who I had let all the way into my heart, every crevasse, every broken crack. This was a woman who I trusted. She spoke the truth, not just to me, she was honest with herself. She had chosen to embrace the truth and love journey that begins within the inward soul. It's the journey that looks straight at the fear you face and walks through it, finding freedom on the other side. I saw in her something incredibly sexy that I longed for, a deep willingness to be vulnerable and face the truth inside herself and value herself enough to work through her issues. I saw she was willing to walk that same journey with me, as I walked the inward truth and love journey of my own. And the more we walked that journey side-by-side, the more we realized that we were walking it as one.

It was time. I filmed her TV segment at 19,000 feet at the summit, then got down on my knee and asked her to make the journey last for the rest of our lives together. I was little nervous when she hesitated, then began to cry. I mustered up the courage and asked one more time, knowing she loved me. The answer, "Yes." No matter how hard the journey in life would be, this was the woman I wanted to walk the truth and love journey with for as long as I would live. There was something that developed over time in our relationship that was the best definition of intimacy we've ever heard. We expressed it often to each other in these simple words, "I see you. I see you, I see all of you, and I embrace you, just as you are." I saw Bethany, and she took my breath away. By the way, she still does today.

Mount Kilimanjaro wouldn't be the hardest summit we'd ever make. We had our marriage ahead, fraught with uncertainties: kids who would struggle with their own fears as we combined our families, possible job losses, and more. But we both now knew, no matter how hard the mountain was to climb, it was in our minds. We had learned how to face our fears, be honest with ourselves and each other, and walk together, always supporting each other.

As we climbed and descended the heights of Mount Kilimanjaro, I realized Bethany and I had stumbled onto one of the most important life lessons you could learn. Life, real life, is experienced in opposites. I've often heard that the Kingdom of God, who He is and what His will is for us, is often experienced with opposite reactions.

What if we could see the world completely differently than we do? What if you saw yourself completely differently than you do?

What if when you failed in life, you learned from it rather than devalued yourself?

What if when you were hurt by someone, you found the courage to forgive them and keep your heart open to love rather than close off the world around you?

What if when you're dealing with a struggle, you are able to share that deep, embarrassing issue with the person you are dating, and you find they accept you rather than shame you? What if you find as you share, they really embrace you as you are?

What if you could share anything, drug issues, porn issues, infidelity desires, and the world's worst thoughts and sins, and that person still loved and embraced you as you are? In truth, that is what Bethany and I discovered our reality to be, because we were reacting to life in the opposite way than most people do. Rather than hide in fear, we faced it and shared. We openly tackled together whatever issue was in front of us, no matter how embarrassing or disappointing it was.

I had spent a lifetime of hiding and I was done with that. As it turns out, Bethany was tired of hiding too. Our friends had told us what not to do, like "Don't share about the affair, don't share what you're really thinking." Instead, we were simply honest, knowing that losing the other would not steal any worth from our own souls. There was peace. There was safety in living in truth and love, and intimacy flourished.

We still have many people today who don't believe us. They don't believe it's possible to share that level of truth and grow closer. But that doubt presupposes you'll be rejected. That doubt is based in fear. Honestly, when they ask us that, we know that doubt oftentimes comes from their own painful experiences of being rejected.

To understand how insidious the world view of protecting our hearts is and how we base all of our relationships on it, consider one of the most common relational phrases of today, "you complete me." This one phrase presupposes we aren't complete without another person. At its core there's a belief that I'm not valuable by myself. This belief causes us to look outward and be driven to find "the one." And if we're getting older, and still haven't found the one, we're driven harder to manipulate situations. We dress up and try to look different than wearing the sweat pants we normally would. Guys, do you really shave every day? Ladies, do you really wear make-up every day? Why not just be the real you and connect in a way where you never have to perform to find "the one."

This world view also causes significant damage in relationships. When we're not happy in our marriage or with our dating partner, how often do we blame them for our unhappiness? Who hasn't thought, "if only you'd do this" or "you don't care about me because you never X (you fill in the blank)." What if we approached life from an opposite way we normally do? What if instead of blaming others for our unhappiness and unfulfillment, we looked inward at what we're struggling with? What if we find healing for the unresolved past pain we've never dealt with? How many relationships have we ended because we looked outward instead of inward? As Demi Moore said at the very end of her book titled *Inside Out,* "The only way out, is in."

Take heart though. Yes, there are times people reject us. There are many, many fears we have. But if we find the courage to keep our hearts open, to do the inward work on our own hearts to find deep peace, then along the journey of life we will find "the one" who embraces us, just as we are.

God sees you, God sees all of you and embraces you, just as you are.

Chapter 19 Reflections—Putting it all together

- Learn to live life in opposites when dealing with your fears, respond in the opposite way. Do what your fears say to run from. As you do that you'll find your capacity for experiencing deep intimate connection grows.

- What if we could see the world completely differently than we do? What if you saw yourself completely differently than you do?

- What if when you failed in life, you learned from it rather than devalued yourself?

- What if when you were hurt by someone, you found the courage to forgive them and keep your heart open to love rather than close off the world around you?

- What if when you're dealing with a struggle, you are able to share that deep, embarrassing issue with the person you are dating, and you find they accept you rather than shame you? What if you find as you share, they really embrace you as you are?

* What if you could share anything, drug issues, porn issues, infidelity desires, and the world's worst thoughts and sins, and that person still loved and embraced you as you are?

Reflections Video: Kilimanjaro Wedding Proposal:
http://bit.ly/kilimanjarowedding

Chapter 20

IT ONLY GETS BETTER—
THE MARRIAGE YEARS

We'd put in so much work during dating, that we were feeling ready for a lifelong celebration. We had, in effect, dated backwards. We did the ugliness of daily life first, then followed up with what we call glamorous marriage. We decided to look at each day of our life as an adventure. We decided we could plan adventures, both large and small, ones that entailed ten minutes to an hour to two hours to a week. We could find adventures that were free, cheap, or expensive depending upon the phase of life we were in or our financial status at that very moment. So, we let the adventures begin. We found that when we wrapped our minds around the life we decided to live, everything changed. We elevated our thinking. We were the Christopher Columbus of our lives and we knew we would find adventure.

A few dozen months after we got married, we found ourselves walking down the cobblestone streets of Rome on a date on our way to the opera. Vince wore a tuxedo, and I wore a long elegant dress that looked like it belonged at the Oscars. We meandered through the busy streets headed to our destination, with passersby stopping us to ask us if we are on our way to get married. "No," we thought, "we're just on a fantastical date. We are creating our own fairy tale. We are speaking together, writing together, and supporting each other in ways that neither of us had ever thought possible. We are sharing brutal truths that are furthering our intimacy, and when we feel like pulling away from each other, we are doing the opposite and pulling closer to one another. We are living in a world of opposites. We are working continually to train ourselves to do the opposite of what we naturally feel drawn to do. The world seems to push us towards isolation when we argue and pull inside ourselves. We fight this natural inclination to do things 'like we've always done them'. We have never had fantastic results in our previous attempts."

Vince had wanted to explore Italy last year, but last year we'd decided on an inexpensive, no-frills hiking trip in Nepal to hike in the Himalayan Mountains. Our budget that year while we were getting our combined debt paid off was small and only allowed our trip to Nepal.

When we combined our lives in marriage, along with it came a burdensome amount of debt that we'd both carried from our previous marriages. This seemed overwhelming to us at first, but we approached it the same way we had the other aspects of our life, truthfully and with love and a plan to tackle it. It has turned out to be the best plan ever as it prepared for a future life unencumbered by debt, allowing us to develop a plan for living our lives together and our plan to build our Dreamscape Retreat in Colorado.

Our $1 a night room in Nepal did not compare to the luxuries of our hotels in Italy. We'd started date nights that were challenges. We'd take a dollar amount that we could save up by cutting things out of our yearly expenditures and then have a "how much can we do with X dollars" dinner planning nights. With our dueling computers it was a bit like watching a game of Yahtzee. "How about a week in the north seeing the Northern Lights—ready, set, go."

We'd each start Googling away to see what we'd come up with for airfare and hotel. "Yuk, way too much money. I'm getting airfares and hotel all-in at X dollars, twice what we have for this next year's budget." And round and round we'd go until we found a destination and an adventure that fit our budget and our desires. The trip to Nepal happened because I fell in love with the pictures on Instagram. "Vince, look at this amazing place called the Annapurna Circuit. There are trails that cover 150 miles around the base of the Himalayan mountains right by Mount Everest." If only we'd known how hard that trek would be. So after two consecutive years of laborious vacations, climbing Mt Kilimanjaro, and hiking 120 miles of the Annapurna Circuit, this year we'd given up dinners out, put off buying the car we needed, stopped going to Starbucks, avoided all clothing stores and shoe stores, and we were on an Italian vacation that was simply fantastic.

It really is hard to believe that this is my life. I've finally reached a place that I'm living my best life and loving every minute of it. Years ago, when I'd hit a life low, I'd embarked on a journey to live my dreams. While embarking on that goal and looking at every aspect of my life, I'd written the book *Live Your Dreams*. I'd interviewed hundreds of people who were not living their best lives. I'd asked each of them why not and what it would take for them to start living their adventure. Many felt too tired to even dream up a new story. It's like being in a dark hole, ten feet below the surface of the earth. In order to get to the next destination, you have to climb out of the hole. In *Live Your Dreams,* I talk through the process of determining where you are and making a plan to begin living your best life. I started the journey that I am on today when I wrote that book. I started the inward journey to discovering my hopes and dreams and needs.

I began working on who I was as a person and why I'd made some of the bad choices in life that I had made. I do agree that the journey starts with an inward journey. I cannot be an incredible life mate if I have not resolved critical pains of my past. I am not complete myself if I'm still harboring resentment and unforgiveness in my heart for a past love. I cannot truly experience life as it was intended for me until I work through what makes me tick. Now that the work was done on my inward journey, Vince had come into my life in a place and a stage where I was ready to take the outward journey to sharing my life with someone cut from a place of peace and rest. I was ready to receive love and accept that I was loveable.

 Every year of marriage to Bethany has been a lifetime of "and they lived happily ever after's." It sounds strange that as a guy I would say this, but I can't think of any other way to describe it. Every year, Bethany and I have experienced more life together, more adventures together, more fulfillment of our purpose, and more peace. To clarify, I'm not saying it's been easy. The pathway to real intimacy requires the effort to communicate, the courage to face possible rejection, the choice to embrace your own value and do the opposite of what fear whispers in your mind. It requires a heart that's willing to be receptive to the other person's insights about your own character weaknesses and to be willing to take the inward journey to understand why you react to situations the way you do.

True intimacy takes you out of your comfort zone to heal and grow. As you grow you will gain wisdom.

It requires a deep commitment.

I'm not referring to the commitment to our spouses we make with the vows "do you take 'blank' to be your wife (husband), to have and to hold from this day forward, for better or worse, for richer, for poorer, in sickness and in health, to love and to cherish, till death do you part?"

Rather it's the harder commitment to walking the Truth and Love journey the rest of your life for yourself first, and then for others. It's the inward journey of being honest with yourself, your Creator, and others. It's the journey in your heart and mind to value yourself as your Creator does, to value your Creator, and to see and treat the others in your life as valuable. That is the commitment that takes relationships that are surviving and makes them thrive. That is the stuff that REAL "happily ever afters" are made from.

I think about the outdoor couch I was sitting on, working on my inward issues with Tammy Kling on a warm summer evening and the words she said, "Vince, I believe you're not supposed to date."

Three weeks later, she told me, "I have someone I want you to meet."

My world was forever changed in those words as Tammy introduced me to the one, a woman I would have never have chosen for myself. I would have written Bethany off as a glossy, superficial executive who was probably more preoccupied with money than with life, honesty, truth, and authentic relationships. Thank God I didn't choose. I'm so incredibly thankful to Tammy for being instrumental in that journey.

To hear Tammy describe it today, on the first day we met face-to-face at her house, God was speaking to her about me and my life. God said don't date. God gave her the name Bethany. Imagine how much He must care for you and I to be in everything we do including dating! Imagine if we just trusted the process and didn't try to control it! Dates would look much different.

First dates with no make-up, sweatpants, and messy hair. First dates of walking the dogs in the rain, getting muddy, and seeing the real person underneath the dirt. Who would have known that you can see someone better with mud on their face than with makeup? We were so unconventional in our approach to dating. I was grateful the woman I was spending time with wasn't the glossy woman I saw in social media. She was real. She was raw. She was a bit crass sometimes, and she was sexy in every part of her soul!

From the first adventure date we took down to Big Bend, Texas, where I received a speeding ticket and Bethany saw the real me react to it to the hike in one of the most gorgeous places in the world, the Kalalau trail, where Bethany saw me throw up from exhaustion, carrying that heavy backpack. Oh, and my feet after walking through rivers, it was the worst smell we had ever smelled.

At the heights of Mount Kilimanjaro at 19,000 feet, Bethany's body was giving out due to the extreme pain she was experiencing from the metal in her spine rubbing into her muscles. This is where the real Bethany was seen when pain erases all patience from conversations. Right before we reached the highest point on the Annapurna Circuit, I remember Bethany sitting down on the ground and giving up. "Just stick a knife in my jugular and get it over with." Luckily, there were some hikers walking by where I could play off her sense of challenge and I said "Oh don't worry, she's a motivational speaker. She'll rally!"

Every ex-spouse interaction, every trying moment with the kids… it was all very difficult sometimes, but we saw life differently having come from a place of losing it all, only to find our own second chance at life and relationships.

Have you had a second-chance moment?

We saw every difficult moment as an opportunity to grow closer to each other. Approaching struggles differently, we did the opposite of duck and cover or attack and belittle the other with weapons. We saw each frustration as an opportunity to share how we were feeling and invite the other into those thoughts, to better understand our own feelings and thoughts and perhaps change them. We also saw it as the opportunity to be deeply vulnerable in the sharing of those thoughts, giving the other the opportunity to really love us in that moment. Understanding how precious those moments were, we were quick to respond in love, providing a listening ear and understanding heart to walk that inward journey with them. In doing so, we created a safe place to share and a deeper bond of connection.

I'm so thankful for the Truth and Love Journey, the journey of the inward soul, and the journey with my incredibly sexy best friend, lover, and one who knows me better than anyone in this world.

 Tears filled my eyes as we drove up the hill. Five years into our relationship, having seen hundreds of relationships changed through the Truth and Love Journey, our dreams and passions were ignited to have a place that would change people's relationships forever.

Set high atop the hill was the most incredibly beautiful cabin retreat I'd ever dreamed of. Now to be honest, I really would have never dreamed that big. I had picked a small plot of land in Colorado in Forbes Park, but God had other plans. As the Spring Fire ravaged so much of Colorado, the land we had picked out burned to the ground. Our selected location for our Dreamscapers Retreat was charred and black like my heart had been only a few short years ago. The land developer who had sold us the land said that he had a beautiful lot in Cripple Creek and offered to swap out our charred land for a spot there. We jumped on a plane to see what we thought of the small town outside of Colorado Springs. It was simply charming. Just fifty miles from the airport of Colorado Springs was the quant town of Cripple Creek. We drove around the mountainous land and drove up and down the roads looking at properties. We drove to the land that the developer had put our name on. It was beautiful. I said, "Vince, let's drive to the top of the mountain," and to the top of the mountain we went. At the top of the hill the view was even more breathtaking.

Sitting right in front of us was a for sale sign and it beckoned us to call the realtor. Okay, so the price was a bit high, and in our minds, we could never imagine a situation where this plot of land would work. It was way over our price range. Vince said, "Bethany, we already have a lot." I don't know why, but I was drawn to this lot, illogically so, high atop the town with the most incredible view of the mountains that I could ever imagine. It was surrounded by Aspen trees. To my left was a cul-de-sac and I saw four deer grazing at the end of the street. It was simply breathtaking.

Somehow, he lowered his price, we came above our desired price and well, we bought the land on the top of that incredible mountain to build the Dreamscapers Retreat. It was actually kind of a crazy idea at the time. What were we thinking? It was wrapped in overwhelming faith since Vince had decided to make a career change. He chose to help people live their dreams through his experience in finances and a holistic wealth management approach. It was the right decision for his career, but nonetheless it left us in a suboptimal cash flow position. On paper, we didn't have the funds to do this. That was another amazing part of our relationship. We didn't always move in a logical direction, but were following a faith journey, true to our purpose and dreams. Like the story in the Bible of the five loaves and two fishes that fed thousands, we were beginning to experience miracles of our own. Leaving behind the scarcity mindset and armed with an understanding that running after our purpose in God's will would allow us to live it, we were driving in a direction we'd never driven before.

When we first started building the cabin, our cash flow on paper was a negative $1800 a month. Writing this down seems a little amusing recognizing that Vince is a financial guy. It was amazing to me that we didn't focus on that. I can't tell you how hard it was to be philanthropic during this time, but we decided that being more giving was who we wanted to be as a couple. We had learned that giving is an important part of continuing to be grateful for all we've been given. We prayed, we trusted God, and a miracle occurred each month. Deals showed up that we didn't anticipate. Vince's financial business began to thrive, and God blessed us. In our own strength and power, we did not believe it was possible. Many times, I had the faith of a mustard seed. When we drove up to that hilltop and saw the completed cabin, I was overwhelmed with seeing our dreams become reality. Is this really real? I looked at Vince and we both felt like we were watching someone else's life. Even more amazing was that God was taking care of every little detail. "Who would manage this property for us?" we thought. And we'd suddenly be introduced to someone who not only would manage it, but they already had renters for us for an upcoming holiday.

The pieces fell into place and it amazed us both. God made a way where we saw no way at all. That has become the one thing that we have seen over and over again. God makes a way when we see no way at all. He has continually blessed us when we are following His will for our lives. He has touched others and given us a purpose and a drive to change other's lives.

And still the adventure is just beginning. Our newest goal is to set thousands of people off on a journey to begin their own truth and love journey. Once we had experienced our own amazing relationship and had seen its positive effects spill over into our relationships with our parents, our children, and our friendships, we began to dream about having a retreat that would touch the sky. We began dreaming of a place where people could come, relax, receive, and begin to learn and discover the keys to great relationships, great sex, and inner peace. For those singles struggling to find the one, we wanted to set them on a course towards their inner journey to fix those precious parts of themselves that hold them back from really finding the person that enhances them, providing fuel on their journey, love, and a newfound acceptance and relief from loneliness that doesn't start from a place of vacancy. For relationships that are struggling in marriages, our desire is to set you off on a better course of life, love, fulfilling sex, acceptance, forgiveness, and deep intimacy.

We are now launching Dreamscaper retreats for couples and singles who are ready to begin their own adventures and enhancements in their lives. We invite you to join us on the Truth and Love Journey. This is your beginning to living both your purpose, finding deep inner peace, and experiencing incredibly deep, vibrant relationships. Your amazing journey awaits! If you're ready to launch into it and not sure how or where to begin, reach out to us. We are excited to help you join a Truth and Love Journey of your own.

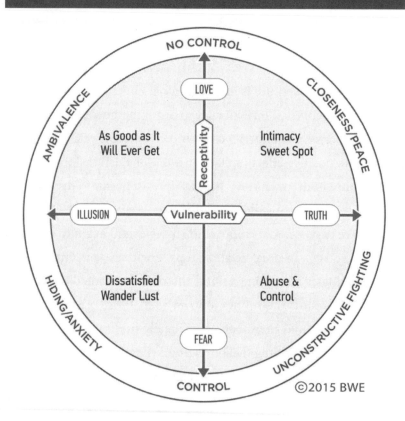

TRUTH & LOVE RELATIONSHIP GRID

Many times we've heard people say, "Just wait, all that great stuff goes away." Does it really have to? We believe it is about energy, focus, planning, attitude, and perspective. Sure, it can go away, yes. But what if you spent time, focus, money and energy on making sure that it did not? What if you spent as much time and energy on your relationship as the world spends on planning and having affairs? What if you decide right now to make it a FOCUSED attention to DO FUN THINGS whether single, dating, married, or widowed? What if you spent time every year planning great getaways and fun things to do to create amazing LIFETASTIC moments? YOU CAN.

Bethany talks about how to do this in her book, *Live Your Dreams*. The best advice we've ever given is to STOP waiting for that special one. Start living the life you want to live right now. If you are dating, be the magnificent person you were born to be and if there is someone for you, and we believe there is, you will find them on this amazing adventure called life.

Start the journey today! Log on to the website www.truthandlovejourney.com, and download the workbook that will start you on the daily journey of living your incredible life. Each day you'll have activities to transform your thinking, your actions, and your life.

Here's a shortened excerpt from our workbook:

Day 1: Every journey starts somewhere. Go back to the pages of the Truth and Love grid. Plot yourself on that grid. Are you living in truth or are illusions more comfortable? Have you been able to hear hard things and listen, evaluate, and accept them? This is a starting point for your amazing journey. You'll find security, peace, and a life partner as you start on this inner journey.

Day 2: Start making a lasting list. What characteristics are you looking for in your mate? What will you desire ten years from now or twenty years from now?

All of this requires that you accept that life is an incredible journey waiting for you to reach out and grab it.

Then, we invite you to go deeper on the journey.

Up in the mountains of Cripple Creek, Colorado, surrounded by gorgeous mountains with a view that is breathtaking, we offer life-giving coaching and retreats to heal your hearts and begin a new journey towards your own Truth and Love Journey. You'll be able to unwind from the responsibilities of life in our secluded #Dreamscapers cabin. Dream again and make an actionable plan for what you want the rest of your life to look like.

Today starts the beginning of an exciting adventure. Let us know how we can help.

Find us on the web at www.truthandlovejourney.com .

Definitions

Fear: The opposite of love, fear keeps us in chains, keeping us from living the truth about what God says about God, other people, and yourselves.

Illusion: The opposite of truth. It is seeing the world from a perspective that ignores obvious truths and creates a view that is not what it is.

Illusionary Living: A life that keeps you from realizing the beauty of who you are and keeps you from living a life of purpose and fulfilling your destiny. Simply put, illusionary living is "less than living."

Intimacy: Being fully known, knowing the other fully, and still being embraced.

Masks: The façades that we create to be loved and adored by others, believing that if we are not something that we create, others will not accept us for who we are.

Soul Wounds: Deep, past emotional wounds that cause us to react to situations in ways that are not in alignment with truth. These often create a PTSD like response that is exaggerated because of past circumstances.

Truths: Accepting truth is believing the following:
  You are loved (just the way you are).
  You are worthy of being loved by others (just the way you are).

You are uniquely and wonderfully made.

You are accepted (with all of your faults, imperfections, missteps, mistakes, past failures, etc).

You have a purpose and a destiny.

You are valuable.

You are full of honor (Isaiah 61:7).

You are made in God's image.

Vulnerability: It is more than being transparent. Being fully vulnerable is revealing deep truths of your fears, your hopes, your insecurities, and your dreams; without holding back, without pre-judging how others will receive those truths, and fully trusting that God is your provider, your ultimate healer and source of affirmation so that you are free to reveal all and live in complete truth. True vulnerability allows you to stop trying to control the situation and to let God be the master of the results.

Weapons: Types of relational weapons used:

• *Silent Treatment*

Silence becomes a deeper weapon that's a punishment that we use to control the other person. We try to punish the other person by not communicating with them. If you feel like you can't trust someone, you often just clam up and refuse to share. The Truth and Love Journey is about taking the risk. It is about being willing to walk the hard road, regardless of you wanting to be silent, it is about opening up and being willing to share. It is about creating an environment of trust so that you become a trustworthy source for sharing.

• *Bringing Up Past Offenses*

It is hard to listen to our faults and listen to factual examples when our faults have hurt those closest to us. That inability to receive constructive criticism often causes us to divert the attention to past offenses that were not really solved. We use these past offenses as a diversionary tactic to shift the focus away from us and, avoid having to deal with the current very painful point that is being brought up about us. Our advice is to receive. This is truly about receptivity. Try to listen. Think about the truth in the statement and reflect on what they are sharing. Be silent. Receive the words without feeling that they at any way reduce your value. You are a valuable creation and having this fault does not diminish your value.

It's important to evaluate why you feel the way you do. Why do you feel the need to divert that attention away from you? There is most probably a painful truth underneath the surface level that you must confront and understand.

• *Changing Topics*

We often use changing topics when we are trying to control others and we don't really want the conversation to go a certain way. You may also have a touch of Attention Deficit Disorder (ADD) and or you haven't truly learned the art of listening.

Focus on why you are changing topics. Are you more focused on yourself than others. It may be a self-centered problem that causes one of us to NOT listen and only want to talk.

This is also a form of diversion. If you are feeling pain from the experience that is being discussed, be prepared to listen and receive. Is there validity in their statements?

• *Guilt Provoking Statements*

Guilt provoking statements are an attempt to control someone through manipulation by using whatever guilting type statements you can create. You try to make the other person feel that they have to do what you want them to do. You are attempting to control the end result by creating an environment that makes the other person feel like they have to do something. When you can release this, you will feel relief. You no longer have to feel bad that they didn't do what you tried to guilt them into doing. You are learning to love them as they are, the way God made them, and allowing Him to make changes to their heart. You will not feel satisfaction in a battle to make him or make her do something.

If we can accept that God our Creator will meet our needs, we can let go of trying to make other people meet our needs.

- *Passive Aggressive Words*

Words and actions that are in your face and camouflage themselves as the hero of the conversation with the intent of shutting down what the other person is saying or asking for and getting your own way is a great explanation of passive aggressive words such as "because you didn't _____, I won't do _____."

They are punishing. Are you trying to punish them? What's the intent of you heart? Unresolved anger, frustration, and pain causes us to indirectly aim to hurt the other person. Our unforgiveness comes out in flippant comments that verbally sound like all is fine when in reality, both people in the conversation can tell that all is not okay.

- *Identity Attacking Statements*

This nuclear weapon cripples your soul and the soul of the one you attack. It's a double-edged knife that cuts both ways. It's the nuclear weapon because it brings total destruction to all around, including yourself. It robs both the sender and the receiver of honor. They feel shame and you take away negative feelings as well. This is a fast track to divorce and breakups. As the most painful and eroding of weapons, it is the equivalent of shooting the other person with a laser guided missile. They are blown to pieces and often will not recover for years to come.

You can recognize identity attacking statements because they are extremes and use the word "you" and mixed with absolute statements. EG "you always, you never, you don't". "You're always going to be a dirtbag."

- *Withholding Sex and Physical Attention*
While we didn't cover this one earlier, this is a commonly used weapon in relationships. Withholding sex as a punishment to manipulate and control the other person is quite often used. Many marriages suffer from this weapon. Any type of manipulation or control is wrong. Sex is a gift that God has given marriage to cement the relationship and develop deep intimacy and relational bonds. Withholding physical attention and sex to punish the other is a power struggle. Allowing yourself to be open to physical contact even when struggling with a relational battle feels very vulnerable. You are releasing control. You are taking away your right to punish them. You are letting God work on their heart and removing yourself as jury and judge in the matter. You are forgiving them for the offense that you are trying to punish them for, even if they haven't asked for forgiveness. You are going on an inward journey to heal, and it isn't conditional upon what they do or don't do. You control you. Eliminating this weapon and opening yourself up to being truly vulnerable in this area of your life will free you to deeper intimacy.

World View: The lens in which you see God, other people, circumstances, and yourself.

Contributions for the Truth and Love Journey

Along the journey, we have been greatly impacted by an amazing group of experts in business, speakers, and authors that are influencing their worlds. As a bonus, we have reached out to these world changers and asked them to answer a key question on relationships: relationships with your family, with your co-workers, and even with yourself. You will be amazed at the depth of their answers and it is our sincere hope that every word in this book blesses you, your life, and forever changes your relationships. A huge debt of gratitude is owed to these incredible humans that bless our lives on a daily basis and were willing to take time out of their busy lives to contribute to your life's success.

Bethany & Vince

The start of a relationship can begin with something as simple as a cell phone text

Ron Hall

Author/Speaker, Celebrity Philanthropist, and Art Dealer

Author of NY Times best-selling book *Same Kind of Different as Me* and movie by the same title

www.RonRHall.com

www.SameKindofDifferentasMeFoundation.org

Q: *How did I take the first step to develop a relationship with someone I didn't know?*

A: With a nice smile I ask "what's your name?" And only once I was told "it ain't none of your business what my name is, I don't tell nobody my name!" He answered in anger as he starred me down with a baseball bat in hand. As it turned out, his name was Suicide and that relationship story is way too long to discuss in a paragraph or two so I wrote a book about it and made it into a movie SAME KIND OF DIFFERENT AS ME.

That said, my first step to my most important relationship was to TEXT......embarrassing, YES. The "Impossible Dream", as I secretly referred to this person, her youthfulness and beauty kept me awake at night wondering how I could possibly connect with her. With unnatural courage, I asked a mutual friend for her cell phone number. Thinking if she saw an unknown number she might not answer, I sent a text. "Hi Beth, this is Ron Hall and you are a "person of interest".

Would you like to spend 5 days in Cabo with me and four other couples? You will have your own room, no hanky panky! I'd just like to get to know you!"

After a good laugh, she texted back "Is this a drunk text"! So in a way, that's how she took her first step.....also, a text! Her next text that immediately followed read, "Person of interest",(is this a criminal investigation, she secretly wondered?) if you are asking me for a date, texting is not an option. Try calling! So, I did.

BTW, we met in Cabo three weeks later, but that is not the whole story. She called back the next morning.

"Well, I'm coming to Cabo and just bought my ticket" she said in a voice that seemed to be from another planet and surely to good to be true.

"I'm so excited, I don't know if I can wait that long to see you. Would you like to go to Paris?" I asked.

"Paris, Texas?"

"No, Paris, France"

"When are you going to Paris?"

"Tomorrow"

"I can't go to Paris tomorrow"

"When can you go to Paris?" I asked, adding that it would the same deal, plane ticket and her own bedroom.

After a short pause, with me wondering if she hung up, she answered "Day after tomorrow!"

Our first date lasted ninety days. We have been together ten years and married nine years.

Now that would make a great book and movie.

So, in my real-life relationships, for my first step, a text worked far better that asking "what's your name!"

The #1 thing anyone can do to improve their relationship with kids, spouse & others- Make a Plan

Gens Johnson

Founder & CEO Gens Johnson Inspires

www.gensjohnson.com

Q: *In such a busy world, what is the one thing anyone can do to improve their relationship with their kids, spouse, and others?*

A: Plan with intention to spend quality time with your family/ loved ones and provide love as frequently as possible.

What you plan to do is what you get done. Family is everything. It's the rich relationships with our family members and loved ones that contribute to the quality and fulfillment of our lives. Since family is a top priority, you have to plan events, meetings, and experiences with them just as you would plan the success of your business.

My advice is to make a 12 Month Plan at the end of each year that includes your family investments; family trips, date nights with your spouse, one on one outings with kids and loved ones, daily, monthly, quarterly, annual efforts.

I have 5 children that are ages 19-24 that live on their own, a husband that travels extensively and 2 aging parents that I am responsible for and love with all my heart.

My 12 Month Plan includes:

1. Daily Prayer. I pray daily for my husband, our marriage, each of our kids, my parents, friends, siblings and other loved ones. The power of prayer is immense and assists me in keeping my priorities straight. It's easy to get caught up in the world. We need a daily plan of attack to stay focused on what we love and value. Daily Touches via text, FaceTime or calls. I intentionally send an inspirational message that will teach and reinforce success principles. I always end with reminding my family how much I love them. It's been my experience in life to grow to your fullest potential you must be in an environment of love. I want to ensure my family always feels loved. What we do daily truly is what makes the biggest impact. Success is in our daily habits.

2. Weekly dates with my husband along with time scheduled several days/week to see my parents and assist them through the transitions of life.

3. Monthly/Quarterly trips with my spouse to visit our children and to bring them together as much as possible throughout the year, whether it's monthly or quarterly depending on everyone's schedule.

4. Asking my family quarterly and annually what I can do to help them. Many times I forget to ask people what they need. I prefer

to give them what I want. Sometimes what I want to give them isn't what they need or want.

5. My husband and I plan an annual family trip and we've recently added our children to our Friend's trip. Increasing the contact and experiences we all share together has not only made our relationships with our kids deeper but it has strengthened the relationships between our kids and our friends.

Since my plan is made prior to the year beginning, with everything added into my annual calendar, all I have to do is execute, impact and enjoy. To me, there sincerely is nothing more important than family. I plan my family's success and I encourage everyone to do the same. Your life will be richer and more meaningful.

The #1 way a leader can improve relationships- Active Listening

Jim Boswell

President & CEO of On Point Healthcare Partners

www.OnPointHealthcarePartners.com

Q: *What's the number one way you feel that a leader could improve relationships?*

A: I think the #1 way leaders could improve relationships is by actively listening with intent to their employees, management team and other stakeholders. By listening to your various stakeholders, a leader gains clarity and insight into current opportunities & challenges.

By listening a leader can gain a different perspective and by a process of deeper questioning & discovery a leader can better determine where to invest his/her time & effort and have confidence he/she has chosen the correct pathway.

One simple factor to build great relationships – Trust

Davene Januszewski

Co-creator of The Master Key Experience

Q: *What's one simple factor that if built will make relationships easier?*

A: Trust: Trust is the currency in relationships that if built, eases the need to work as hard at them. We see that if there's conflict in a personal or business relationship, its due to a lack of trust. If each person fully trusts the other, each person inherently knows the other has their best interests at heart. Once trust is built then each can easily believe that they are getting the better part of the interactions and the relationship.

One thing that inhibits successful relationships from a Psychologist's perspective-Setting expectations too high

Dr. Shannan Crawford

Psychologist, Speaker, Author

www.drshannancrawford.com

Q: *With relationships being immensely valuable, what is 1 thing that you see are inhibiting people from developing healthy relationships, from your professional view point?*

A: I would say: Disappointment from unmet expectations.

In which we create an internal rule book, with the illusion that our spouse/partner "should" satisfy all of our needs and "always" be there for us, understand us, champion us, and support us. This view is unrealistic and often the expectations themselves are not stated so our partner does not know they are being held to those unstated expectations.

Developing healthy relationships in a competitive workplace environment

John Patterson

Author, Former Major League Baseball Pitcher, Father, Husband

www.perspectiveagent.com

Q: *How can you have healthy relationships in a competitive work-place environment?*

A: To me, a competitive workplace environment is created when you're surrounded by people who have had a lot of success in their life. It looks like working with people who graduated at the top of their class, maybe from an Ivey league school, and who are top in their field. To get the best of yourself and get the best out of those around you, I've found you have to lead by example and not allow the competitive environment to take away from the team. I learned this early on when I went from a small pond to a big pond and found I was surrounded by like-minded competitive people. I learned the best way to overcome a competitive workplace environment, where authentic relationships are second to success, is to show respect, compliment and see the good in others. Giving respect to another person rubs off on others who in turn show respect to others. It changes the environment you're in.

If you're trying to build a healthy relationship, you're not going to do that by competing with someone. You might get some respect from successfully accomplishing a task or project. But that's not going to build a healthy lasting relationship. Building a real friendship in the workplace starts with focusing on the team and focusing on getting the best out of others.

In my career as a major league baseball pitcher, I learned having a professional relationship didn't create lasting friendships. It was only the people I was open to, honest and vulnerable with, whom I showed value to, that I built a strong friendship with that's lasted beyond my professional baseball career.

Successfully creating relationships that accomplish business goals.

Ron Lusk

Investor & Director at several companies

Q: *What is the hardest relationship challenge you've had in negotiating and landing some of your biggest deals?*

A: The most difficult challenge in any transaction is assembling the team with people that possess the proper skill sets to accomplish the goal. In fact, I was doing an interview yesterday on this very topic with a college business student, the son of dear friends of ours whose mother is a veterinarian. I asked him: if your dog were sick would you take him to a bus driver or your mother? Often times the most obvious solution to problems are overlooked due to failure of leadership to assemble the right team in favor of yielding to current management. Of course, the correct answer is the veterinarian. How many times are we creating the relationship with the wrong team or a person that cannot accomplish the goal?

I once had a very large transaction that was stuck on an issue that legal counsel for our side didn't quite understand. He was offended when I suggested that we bring in a subject matter expert. We dismissed from the team. After the transaction closed, he called, and we went to lunch. He said, "I learned a very valuable lesson that day". To this day he still represents me and is the first to bring in others with more knowledge than he possesses. My Grandmother always said, "we can make money with a hole in the ground if we have someone that knows how to run it". Find the right resources, develop the relationship, and you'll find increased success in your business goals.

Are you listening or just wanting to talk?

Bruce Pulver

Author and Speaker

www.abovethechatterourwordsmatter.com

Q: *Are you listening, or just waiting to talk? Can we learn to listen for understanding versus listening to respond, align, argue or fix?*

A: Many times in relationships, the risk of blowups, breakups and screwups is high. I vote for improving our LISTENING commitment and skills.

One of the most impactful questions, I ever encountered about relationships and communication was:

Are you listening, or just waiting to talk? Can we learn to listen for understanding versus listening to respond, align, argue or fix?

Diving deep into this question, I found it permeates through both professional and personal relationships and in all stages (introduction, development, maturity, sustaining).

Listening is an active behavior that calls for less action in most cases than responding invokes. For someone to feel connected to and heard by another person, the call for an immediate response must be put on pause and replaced with a question or empathetic response that allows the other person space and time to explain, explore and expound on their topic, question, issue or concern.

Can you tell me more? I can understand why you might think or feel that way. Can you give me some additional insight? What do you believe has caused this situation?

Fixing is often NOT listening. A structured "do this" or "stop doing that" falls short of intentional listening and prevents real connection in relationships. The skilled and caring listener often can help the other person arrive at his/her own solution and feel stronger/encouraged by the encounter.

The relationship between the two when the listening is active, supporting, engaging and encouraging grows stronger.

Is active listening easy? No! Is it worth the effort? Absolutely.

A successful relationship starts with great thoughts, and then totally surrender to the relationship

Mark Januszewski

The World's Laziest Networker, Kauai

www.worldslaziestnetworker.com

A thousand different people will give you a 1000 different answers about what makes a successful relationship. Most likely, they all will make some sense. Deeper dives into relationships will reveal something quite different. Most of the answers to what makes for great, meaningful relationships come from pain, most lessons learned you arrive at from what didn't work. Planning against mistakes, planning to avoid pain, planning to avoid hurt is not planning for success, fulfillment and intimacy.

So many times, I've bought books, went to seminars for business and for personal development and was told it is all about relationships. Then? I heard nothing but platitudes, hopes and words like "empower" and "honor" without a single suggestion about how to do it. Through trail and success, I've come to understand that if you want to build something great you must begin with great thoughts... not of past failures. That is step one. Step two is to surrender, totally surrender to the relationship… it becomes bigger than both parties, a third entity if you will. Unless the personal agendas are set aside, the relationship can never come first. If it does not come first, then it is merely an "arrangement" masquerading as a "relationship" that is doomed before it really begins.

The key here, of course, is trust. Both parties, whether business, personal or the deepest of intimate relationships, are dependent upon the building of trust. All decisions must be made with respect to the best interests of the relationship. Here's where it gets tricky… and where greatness lurks. While the relationship must be the respected part of all decisions, the individual's individualism must be encouraged so growth to all 3 is mandated. Sound interesting? It is magic and no one can help you navigate this incredible terrain better than Bethany and Vince. Pure magic.